The ESOP Reader

2003 Edition

Edited by Scott Rodrick and Corey Rosen

The National Center for Employee Ownership • Oakland, CA

The ESOP Reader, 2003 Edition (3rd ed.)
Edited by Scott Rodrick and Corey Rosen
Book design by Scott Rodrick

ISBN: 0-926902-86-5

First printing: December 2002

The National Center for Employee Ownership
1736 Franklin St., 8th Flr.
Oakland, CA 94612
(510) 208-1300
Fax (510) 272-9510
Email *nceo@nceo.org*
Web *www.nceo.org*

Contents

Preface

Corey Rosen

The ESOP Reader is the NCEO's most venerable publication. This edition, completely revised as of October 2002, is one in a long line of revisions of a book that goes back to our founding in 1981. Back then, employee ownership was an unknown and somewhat suspect notion. Today, we estimate that 25 to 30 million Americans own stock in their company through one kind of plan or another. About 8.5 million of these are participants in an employee stock ownership plan (ESOP), the oldest and most successful form of broad-based employee ownership.

ESOPs are the beneficiaries of some very special tax benefits, reflecting support that Congress has given this idea since the law was established in 1974. Contributions to ESOPs are tax-deductible to the company, but not taxable to the employee until the employee gets a distribution of the shares after terminating employment. ESOPs can borrow money and repay it in pretax corporate dollars. Provided certain basic rules are met, sellers to ESOPs can defer capital gains taxes on the proceeds of the sale. ESOPs that own stock in S corporations do not pay tax on their share of corporate earnings, meaning that 100% ESOP S corporation ESOPs pay no federal income tax. That's by law, not by some legal loophole.

In return for these benefits, companies must comply with a variety of rules to ensure the benefits of an ESOP are equitably distributed. ESOPs are not a way to provide for discretionary awards of stock to employees. They are also not ways to concentrate benefits in the hands of a few people while leaving a smaller amount to be distributed to everyday workers. Most of these rules are the same as for other retirement-type plans, such as profit sharing and 401(k) plans, however, so they should not be especially onerous to most well-meaning companies.

ESOPs are often misunderstood. They are often confused with stock option plans, which are another animal altogether. They are not stock purchase plans; employees almost never buy stock through an ESOP. They do not require that employees run the company or even elect the board, unless companies want to structure themselves that way. Most people, in fact, would be well served by forgetting what they have heard or thought about ESOPs before starting to learn more about them.

What's most important about ESOPs, though, is that they really seem to work. Companies with ESOPs grow faster, have higher productivity, and compensate employees better than would be expected without their plans. Companies that combine employee ownership with what we call an "ownership culture" do especially well. These companies really work to make people feel like owners. They share corporate and work-level performance information, and they organize employees into teams that have increased authority to make decisions about work-level issues. They actively seek out and listen to employee input. They show employees they value them as people, not just "assets." These companies grow much faster after their ESOPs are implemented than more conventionally managed businesses, and even conventionally managed ESOP companies.

Done well, then, ESOPs are a strategy that can enrich the lives of business owners and employees. That enrichment is not just financial. It also comes from the dignity of being treated well, the satisfaction of doing the right thing, and the opportunity to learn and grow. We hope this book will help companies achieve all of this.

CHAPTER 1

An Overview of ESOPs

Corey Rosen

On a rainy business trip to Florida recently, I got up early and put on my Gore-Tex running outfit to go out for my morning jog. After showering, I threw my Crest Toothpaste into a bag and hurried over to Starbucks for coffee and a pastry. I needed to catch my Southwest Airlines flight soon, but I left my razor at home, so I rushed into the Publix Supermarket and picked one up. It was going to be a long day, but I felt good that all the products and services I'd used so far had come from companies where the employees were substantial or principal owners.

I have to say my story is made up, but it could have happened. What has happened to employee ownership, however, is very real. There are now over 20 million employees who own stock in their companies through employee stock ownership plans (ESOPs), 401(k) plans with heavy concentrations of employer stock, broadly granted stock options, or stock purchase plans.

For various reasons, ESOPs have been a major part of this trend for many years. ESOPs provide attractive tax benefits. They allow companies to borrow money and repay it in pretax dollars. They provide a way for owners of closely held businesses to sell all or part of their interests and defer taxation on the gain. And they make it possible for companies to provide an employee benefit simply by contributing tax-deductible shares of their own stock, among other benefits. Just as important, however, are potential productivity gains. Studies consistently show that when broad employee ownership is combined with a highly participative management style, companies perform much better than they otherwise would be expected to do. Neither ownership nor participation accomplishes these significant gains on its own. Companies want employees to "think and act like owners." What better way to do that than to make them owners? Finally, employees are beginning to expect equity, at least in some sectors.

As of December 2002, there were about 11,500 ESOPs in the U.S. covering over 8.5 million participants and controlling about $500 billion in assets. Of these, about 5% are in publicly traded companies and 95% in closely held companies. The median percentage ownership for ESOPs in public companies is about 10% to 15%. Most public companies maintain an ESOP along with other benefit plans. The median ownership percentage for private companies is about 30% to 40%, and about 3,000 companies are majority employee-owned. While the typical company has 20 to 500 employees, employees own a majority of the stock of such companies as Lifetouch (15,000 employees), TTC, Inc. (30,000 employees), Publix Supermarkets (109,000 employees), and Science Applications (39,000 employees). About half the ESOPs in private companies are used to buy out an owner; the rest are typically used as a primary employee benefit plan, sometimes in conjunction with borrowing money for capital acquisition.

While ESOPs are the main vehicle for employee ownership, 401(k) plans are not far behind. By 2000, these plans owned about $250 billion in company stock, primarily in public companies. Based on various recent surveys, it appears about 60% of the corporate matching funds in public company 401(k) plans is in company stock, with a much smaller percentage in private companies. Public company employees can usually choose to buy shares in their own company 401(k) plans as well. Overall, in 2002, about 18% of all 401(k) assets were in the form of employer stock. While these plans own a great deal of company stock, they rarely own more than 10% of any one company, and few companies with employer stock in 401(k) plans really think of themselves as "employee ownership" companies. A number of companies combine their 401(k) and ESOP plans into "KSOPs," and some very small companies find that a 401(k) with a company match is more convenient and economical than an ESOP, so this chapter also addresses how 401(k) plans work.

How ESOPs Work

An ESOP is a kind of employee benefit plan. Governed by ERISA (the Employee Retirement Income Security Act), ESOPs were given a specific statutory framework in 1974. In the ensuing 12 years, they were given a number of other tax benefits. Like other qualified deferred compensation plans, they must not discriminate in their operation in favor of highly compensated employees, officers, or owners. To assure that these rules are met, ESOPs must appoint a trustee to act as the plan fiduciary. This can be anyone, although larger companies tend to appoint an outside trust institution, while smaller companies typically appoint a manager or create an ESOP trust committee.

The most sophisticated use of an ESOP is to borrow money (a "leveraged" ESOP). In this approach, the company sets up a trust. The trust then borrows money from a lender. The company repays the loan by making tax-deductible contributions to the trust, which the trust gives to the lender. The loan must be used by the trust to acquire stock in the company. Proceeds from the loan can be used by the company for any legitimate business purpose. The stock is put into a "suspense account," where it is released to employee accounts as the loan is repaid. However, for purposes of calculating the various contribution limits described below, the employee is considered to have received only his or her share of the principal paid that year, not the value of the shares released. After employees leave the company or retire, the company distributes to them the stock purchased on their behalf, or its cash value. In practice, banks often require a second step in the loan transaction of making the loan to the company instead of the trust, with the company reloaning the proceeds to the ESOP.

In return for agreeing to funnel the loan through the ESOP, the company gets a number of tax benefits, provided it follows the rules to assure employees are treated fairly. First, the company can deduct the entire loan contribution it makes to the ESOP, within certain payroll-based limits described below. That means the company can, in effect, deduct interest and principal on the loan, not just interest. Second, the company can deduct dividends paid on the shares acquired with the proceeds of the loan that are used to repay the loan itself (in other words, the earnings of the stock being acquired help pay for the stock itself). Again, there are limits, as described below in sections on the rules of the loan and contribution limits.

The ESOP can also be funded directly by discretionary corporate contributions or cash to buy existing shares or simply by the contribution of shares. These contributions are tax-deductible, generally up to 25% of the total eligible payroll of plan participants.

ESOP Applications

The ESOP can buy both new and existing shares, for a variety of purposes.

- The most common application for an ESOP is *to buy the shares of a departing owner of a closely held company.* Owners can defer tax on the gain they have made from the sale to an ESOP if the ESOP holds more than 30% of the company's stock (and certain other requirements are met). Moreover, the purchase can be made in pretax corporate dollars.

- ESOPs are also used *to divest or acquire subsidiaries, buy back shares from the market (including public companies seeking a takeover defense), or restructure existing benefit plans* by replacing current benefit contributions with a leveraged ESOP.

- The use of ESOPs first envisioned by ESOP creator Louis Kelso was *to buy newly issued shares in the company, with the borrowed funds being used to buy new capital.* The company can, in effect, finance growth or acquisitions in pretax dollars while these same dollars create an employee benefit plan.

- The above uses generally involve borrowing money through the ESOP, but a company can simply contribute new shares of stock to an ESOP, or cash to buy existing shares, *as a means to create an employee benefit plan.* As more and more companies want to find ways to tie employee and corporate interests, this is becoming a more popular application. In public companies especially, an ESOP contribution is often used as part or all of a match to employee deferrals to an 401(k) plan.

Rules for ESOP Loans

ESOPs are unique among benefit plans in that they can borrow money. Typically, a lender will loan to the company, with the company reloaning the money to the ESOP. The ESOP then uses the loan proceeds to buy new or treasury shares of stock (when the ESOP is used to finance growth) or existing shares (when the ESOP is used to buy shares of current owners). Of course, the ESOP itself does not have any money to repay the loan, so the company makes tax-deductible contributions to the plan that the plan then uses to repay the lender. This means, in effect, the company can deduct principal and interest on the loan, provided the requirements described below are met.

The ESOP can borrow money from anyone, including commercial lenders, sellers of stock, or even the company itself. Any loan to an ESOP must meet several requirements, however. The loan must have reasonable rates and terms and must be repaid only from employer contributions, dividends on shares in the plan, and earnings from other investments in the trust contributed by the employer. There is no limit on the term of an ESOP loan other than what lenders will accept (normally five to ten years), and the proceeds from the sale of shares to the ESOP can be used for any business purpose.

Shares in the plan are held in a suspense account. As the loan is repaid, these shares are released into the accounts of plan participants. The release must follow one of two formulas. The simplest is that the percentage of shares released equals the percentage of principal paid, either that year or during whatever shorter repayment period is used. In such cases, however, the release may not be slower than what normal amortization schedules would provide for a 10-year loan with level payments of principal and interest. The principal only method usually has the effect of releasing fewer shares to participants in the early years. Alternatively, the company can base its release on the total amount of principal and interest it pays each year. This method can be used for any loan, but it must be used for loans of over 10 years.

In either case, it is important to remember that the value of the shares released each year is rarely the same as the amount contributed to repay the principal on the loan. If the price of the shares goes up, the amount released will be higher, in dollar terms, than the amount contributed; if it goes down, the dollar value of the amount released will be lower. The amount *contributed* to repay the principal on the loan is what counts for determining if the company is within the limits for contributions allowed each year and for the purpose of calculating the tax deduction. The value of the shares released, however, is the amount used on the income statement, where it counts as a compensation cost.

Limitations on Contributions

In 2001, Congress made significant changes to contribution limits in all employee retirement plans. The discussion below describes how plans now operate, under rules that became effective as of January 1, 2002. At the end of this section, the major differences under prior law are described.

First, it is important to understand that in a leveraged ESOP, the amount the company is considered to have contributed to the ESOP, or that is defined as an "annual addition" to an employee's account, is based on the amount of principal paid off each year attributable to each employee's account. The actual addition to an employee's account, however, is the value of the shares released, but this value is not the one used for contribution and annual addition testing.

Congress was generous in providing tax benefits for leveraged ESOPs, but there are limits. Generally, companies can deduct up to 25% of the total eligible payroll of plan participants to cover the principal portion of the loan and can deduct all of the interest income they pay. Eligible pay is essentially all the pay, including employee deferrals into benefit plans, of people actually in the plan, of $200,000 per participant or less (in 2002 dollars). However, company contributions to other defined contribution plans, such as stock bonus, 401(k), or profit sharing plans, must be counted in this 25% of pay calculation. On the other hand, "reasonable" dividends paid on shares acquired by the ESOP loan can be used to repay the loan, and these are not included in the 25% of pay calculations. If employees leave the company before they have a fully vested right to their shares, their forfeitures, which are allocated to everyone else, are not counted in the percentage limitations. If the ESOP does not borrow money, the annual contribution limit is now also 25% of covered pay (it had been 15% under the old law). Again, contributions to other plans reduce this amount.

There are several limitations to these provisions, however. First, no one ESOP participant can receive a contribution of more than 100% of pay in any year from the principal payments on the loan that year that are attributable to that employee, or more than $40,000 (a number that will be indexed for inflation in $1,000 increments), whichever is less. In figuring payroll, pay over $200,000 per year (in 2002 dollars) does not count towards total contribution limits. Second, if there are other qualified benefit plans, these must be taken into account when assessing this limit. This means that employee deferrals into 401(k) plans, as well as other employer contributions to 401(k) plans, stock bonus, or profit sharing plans, are added to the ESOP contribution and cannot exceed 100% of pay in any year.

Third, the interest is excludable from the 25% of pay individual limit only if not more than one-third of the benefits are allocated to highly compensated employees, as defined by the Internal Revenue Code (section 414 (q)). If the one-third rule is not met, forfeitures are also counted in determining how much an employee is getting each year. If the company sponsoring the ESOP is an S corporation, interest is also not deductible.

The rules described above apply for plan years after December 31, 2001. Prior rules were much more restrictive with respect to contribution limitations. The major differences are as follows:

- The limit on employer contributions in non-leveraged plans was only 15% of pay. "Pay" was defined to exclude employee deferrals into 401(k) plans (now it is included).

- The limitation on how much can be added to an employee account each year from employer contributions and employee deferrals was 25% of pay.

- Pay over $170,000 (the 2001 equivalent of the $200,000 figure above) was not defined as "eligible pay" for contribution limits.

Using Dividends to Repay the Loan

The 1986 tax act allowed companies to take a tax deduction when using "reasonable" dividend payments to repay the ESOP loan. These payments do not count against the contribution limits described above. While the term "reasonable" has never been defined, most consultants believe it is a percentage of share value consistent with what other companies in the industry would pay given similar levels of profits. Many companies are using preferred stock in their ESOPs to allow for higher dividend payments. Whatever kind of stock is used, the amount of the dividends must be allocated to employee accounts. Companies normally allocate these amounts in the form of shares released from the suspense account.

Companies can also "pass through" dividends directly to employees. Typically, companies would pay dividends on allocated shares (whether in a leveraged or non-leveraged plan). These dividends are also tax-deductible to the company. Finally, dividends that are voluntarily reinvested by the employee back into company stock in the ESOP are also tax-deductible to the company. It is possible to combine this arrangement with a 401(k) plan in such a way that the employee can do this on a pretax basis, something that is done mostly in publicly traded companies.

How Shares Get to Employees

The rules for ESOPs are similar to the rules for other tax-qualified plans in terms of participation, allocation, vesting, and distribution, but several special considerations apply. Generally speaking, all employees over age 21 who work for more than 1,000 hours in a plan year must be included in the plan, unless they are covered by a collective bargaining unit, are in a separate line of business with at least 50 employees not covered by the ESOP, or fall into one of several anti-discrimination exemptions not commonly used by leveraged ESOPs. If there is a union, the company must bargain in good faith with it over inclusion in the plan.

Shares are allocated to individual employee accounts based on relative compensation (generally, all W-2 compensation is counted), on a more level formula (such as per capita or seniority), or some combination. The allocated shares are subject to vesting. Employees must be 100% vested after five years of service, or the company can use a graduated vesting schedule not slower than 20% after three years and 20% per year more until 100% is reached after seven years. A faster vesting schedule applies where the ESOP contribution is used as a match to employee 401(k) deferrals. In such cases, "cliff" vesting must be complete in three years and graduated vesting must start after two years and be completed no later than after six years.

When employees reach age 55, and have 10 years of participation in the plan, the company must either give them the option of diversifying 25% of their account balances among at least three other investment alternatives, or simply pay the amount out to the employees. At age 60, employees can have 50% diversified or distributed to them.

When employees retire, die, or are disabled, the company must distribute their vested shares to them not later than the last day of the plan year following the year of their departure. For employees leaving before reaching retirement age, distribution must begin not later than the last day of the sixth plan year following their year of separation from service. Payments can be in substantially equal installments out of the trust over five years, or in a lump sum. In the installment method, a company normally pays out a portion of the stock from the trust each year. The value of that stock may go up or down over that time, of course. In a lump sum distribution, the company buys the shares at their current value, but can make the purchase in installments over five years, as long as it provides adequate security and reasonable interest. ESOP shares must be valued at least annually by an independent outside appraiser unless the shares are publicly traded.

Closely held companies and some thinly traded public companies must repurchase the shares from departing employees at their fair market value, as determined by an independent appraiser. This so-called "put option" can be exercised by the employee in one of two 60-day periods, one starting when the employee receives the distribution and the second period one year after that. The employee can choose which one to use. This obligation should be considered at the outset of the ESOP and factored into the company's ability to repay the loan.

Voting Rules

Voting is one of the most controversial and least understood ESOP issues. The trustee of the ESOP actually votes the ESOP shares. The question is "who directs the trustee?" The trustee can make the decision independently, although that is very rare. Alternatively, management or the ESOP administrative committee can direct the trustee, or the trustee can follow employee directions.

In private companies, employees must be able to direct the trustee

as to the voting of shares *allocated* to their accounts on several key issues, including closing, sale, liquidation, recapitalization, and other issues having to do with the basic structure of the company. They do not,
however, have to be able to vote for the board of directors or on other
typical corporate governance issues, although companies can voluntarily provide these rights. Instead, the plan trustee votes the shares, usually at the direction of management. In listed corporations, employees
must be able to vote on all issues.

Voting rights are more complicated than they seem. First, voting is
not the same as tendering shares. So while employees may be required
to vote on all issues, they may have no say about whether shares are tendered. In public companies, this is a major issue. Almost all public companies now write their plans to give employees the right to direct the
tendering, as well as voting, of their shares, for reasons to be explained
below.

Second, employees are not required to be able to vote on unallocated
shares. In a leveraged ESOP, this means that for the first several years
of the loan, the trustee can vote the majority of the shares, if that is what
the company wants to do. The company could provide that unallocated
shares, as well as any allocated shares for which the trustee has not received instructions, should be voted or tendered in proportion to the
allocated shares for which directions were received.

What this all means is that for almost all ESOP companies, governance is not really an issue unless they want it to be. If companies want
employees to have only the most limited role in corporate governance,
they can; if they want to go beyond this, they can as well. In practice,
companies that do provide employees with a substantial governance role
find that it does not result in dramatic changes in the way the company
is run.

Valuation

In closely held companies and some thinly traded listed companies, all
ESOP transactions must be based on a current appraisal by an independent, outside valuation expert. The valuation process assesses how much
a willing buyer would pay a willing seller for the business. This calculation is performed by looking at various ratios, such as price-to-earnings,

at discounted future cash flow and earnings, at asset value, and at comparable companies, among other things. It is then adjusted to reflect whether the sale is for control (owning a controlling interest in a business is worth more than owning a minority interest, even on a per share basis) and marketability (shares of public companies are worth more than closely held companies because they are easier to buy and sell). ESOP company shares have better marketability than non-ESOP companies, however, because the ESOP provides a market, albeit not as active a one as a stock exchange.

Tax Benefits to the Selling Shareholder

One of the major benefits of an ESOP for closely held companies is section 1042 of the Internal Revenue Code. Under it, a seller to an ESOP may be able to qualify for a deferral of taxation of the gain made from the sale. Several requirements apply, the most significant of which are:

1. The seller must have held the stock for three years before the sale.

2. The stock must not have been acquired through stock options or other employee benefit plans.

3. The ESOP must own 30% or more of the value of the shares in the company and must continue to hold this amount for three years unless the company is sold. Shares repurchased by the company from departing employees do not count. Stock sold in a transaction that brings the ESOP to 30% of the total shares qualifies for the deferral treatment.

4. Shares qualifying for the deferral cannot be allocated to the ESOP accounts of the selling shareholder(s); children, brothers or sisters, spouses, or parents of the selling shareholder(s); or to any more-than-25% shareholders (not just selling shareholders).

5. The company must be a C corporation.

If these rules are met, the seller (or sellers) can take the proceeds from the sale and reinvest them in "qualified replacement securities" within 12 months after the sale or three months before and defer any capital gains tax until these new investments are sold. Qualifying replacement securities are defined essentially as stocks, bonds, warrants, or debentures of domestic corporations receiving not more than 25% of their income from passive investment. Mutual funds and real estate trusts do not qualify. If the replacement securities are held until death, they are subject to a step-up in basis, so capital gains taxes would never be paid.

Increasingly, lenders are asking for replacement securities as part or all of the collateral for an ESOP loan. This strategy may be beneficial to sellers selling only part of their holdings because it frees the corporation to use its assets for other borrowing and could enhance the future value of the company.

It is also important to note that people taking advantage of the "1042" treatment cannot have stock reallocated to their accounts from these sales if they remain employees. Other 25% shareholders and close relatives of the seller also cannot receive allocations from these sales.

Financial Issues for Employees

When an employee receives a distribution from the plan, it is taxable unless rolled over into an IRA or other qualified plan. Otherwise, the amounts contributed by the employer are taxable as ordinary income, while any appreciation on the shares is taxable as capital gains. In addition, if the employee receives the distribution before normal retirement age and does not roll over the funds, a 10% excise tax is added.

While the stock is in the plan, however, it is not taxable to employees. It is rare, moreover, for employees to give up wages to participate in an ESOP or to purchase stock directly through a plan (this raises difficult securities law issues for closely held companies). Most ESOPs either are in addition to existing benefit plans or replace other defined contribution plans, usually at a higher contribution rate.

Determining ESOP Feasibility

Several factors are involved in determining whether a company is a good ESOP candidate:

*   *Is the cost reasonable?* ESOPs typically cost $20,000 and up, depending on complexity and the size of the transaction. This is usually

much cheaper than other ways to sell a business, but more expensive than other benefit plans.

- *Is the payroll large enough?* Limitations on how much can be contributed to a plan may make it impractical to use an ESOP to buy out a major owner or finance a large transaction. For instance, a $5 million purchase would not be feasible if the company has $500,000 of eligible payroll because annual contributions could be no larger than $125,000 (25%) per year, not enough to repay a loan for that amount. It may be possible to go over this amount somewhat, however, through the use of deductible dividends. Companies can also set up the loan so that the bank lends to the company on one term (say seven years) and the company reloans the money to the ESOP on another (say 12 years), meaning that the principal payments are stretched out longer and the percentage of pay required each year is smaller.

- *Can the company afford the contributions?* Many ESOPs are used to buy existing shares, a non-productive expense. Companies need to assess whether they have the available earnings to cover this.

- *Is management comfortable with the idea of employees as owners?* While employees do not have to run the company, they will want more information and more say after an ESOP is implemented. Unless they are treated this way, research shows, they are likely to be demotivated by ownership.

The ESOP Repurchase Obligation

One of the major issues closely held ESOP companies must face is the obligation to provide for repurchasing the shares of departing employees. The legal obligation rests with the company, although it can fund this by making tax-deductible contributions to the ESOP, which the ESOP uses to repurchase the shares. Most companies either do this or buy the shares back themselves and then recontribute them to the ESOP (and take a tax deduction for that). Either way, shares continue to circulate in the plan, providing stock for new employees. Some companies, however, buy back the shares and retire them or have other people buy them (a manager, for instance).

The repurchase obligation may seem like a reason not to do an ESOP ("You mean we have to buy back the shares continually?" people often ask). In fact, all closely held companies have a 100% repurchase obligation at all times. An ESOP simply puts it on a schedule and allows the company to do it with pretax dollars. Nonetheless, the repurchase obligation can be a major problem if companies do not anticipate and plan for it. A careful repurchase study should be conducted periodically to help manage this process.

ESOPs in S Corporations

ESOPs can now own stock in S corporations. While these ESOPs operate under most of the same rules as in a C corporation, there are important differences. First, interest payments on ESOP loans count towards the contribution limits (they normally do not in C companies). Dividends paid on ESOP shares are also not deductible. Second, and most importantly, sellers to an ESOP in an S corporation do not qualify for the tax-deferred rollover treatment. (There used to be another difference: for plan years before January 1, 2002, the annual limit on contributions was 15% of pay per year, although the ESOP could be combined with a money purchase plan to reach the 25% limit.)

On the other hand, the ESOP is unique among S corporation owners in that it does not have to pay federal income tax on any profits attributable to it (state rules will vary). This can make an ESOP very attractive in some cases. It also makes converting to an S corporation very appealing when a C corporation ESOP owns a high percentage of the company's stock.

For owners who want to use an ESOP to provide a market for their shares, generally it will make sense to convert to C status before setting up an ESOP. Where selling shares is not a priority, or where the seller either does not have substantial capital gains taxes due on the sale or has other reasons to prefer staying an S corporation, an S ESOP can provide significant tax benefits. However, owners must keep in mind that any distributions paid to owners must be paid pro-rata to the ESOP. The ESOP can use these distributions to purchase additional shares, to build up cash for future repurchases of employee shares, or just to add to employee accounts.

While the S corporation rules make an ESOP very attractive, legislation passed in 2001 makes it clear that these rules are not meant to be abused by companies seeking to create the ESOP primarily to benefit a few people. For instance, some accountants were promoting plans in which a company would set up an S corporation management company owned by just a few people that would manage a large C corporation. The profits would flow through the S corporation, which would then not be taxed.

The rules Congress enacted are complicated, but they boil down to two essential points. First, people who own more than 10% of all company stock (including shares allocated in the ESOP, synthetic equity such as stock options, and directly owned shares), or who own 20% counting their family members, are considered "disqualified" persons. ESOP ownership is defined to include synthetic equity as well, such as stock options. Second, if these disqualified people together own more than 50% of the company's shares (counting their synthetic equity), then they cannot get allocations in the ESOP without extraordinary tax penalties. Congress also directed the IRS to apply this onerous tax treatment to any plan it deems to be substantially for the purpose of evading taxes rather than providing employee benefits.

Steps to Setting Up an ESOP

If you have decided an ESOP is worth investigating, there are several steps to take to implement a plan. At each point, you may decide you have gone far enough and that an ESOP is not right for you.

1. *Determine whether other owners are amenable.* This may seem like an obvious issue, but sometimes people take several of the steps listed below before finding out if the existing owners are willing to sell. Employees should not start organizing a buyout unless they have some reason to think the parent firm is willing to sell (it may not be, for instance, if its goal is to reduce total output of a product it makes at other locations). Or there may be other owners of a private firm who will never agree to an ESOP, even if it seems appealing to the principal owners. They could cause a good deal of trouble down the road.

2. *Conduct a feasibility study.* This may be a full-blown analysis by an
    outside consultant, replete with market surveys, management inter-
    views, and detailed financial projections, or it may simply be a care-
    ful business plan performed in-house. Generally, full-scale feasibil-
    ity studies are only needed when there is some doubt about the
    ESOP's ability to repay the loan. Any analysis, however, must look
    at several items. First, it must assess just how much extra cash flow
    the company has available to devote to the ESOP, and whether this
    is adequate for the purposes for which the ESOP is intended. Sec-
    ond, it must determine if the company has adequate payroll for ESOP
    participants to make the ESOP contributions deductible. Remem-
    ber to include the effect of other benefit plans that will be main-
    tained in these calculations. Third, estimates must be made of what
    the repurchase liability will be and how the company will handle it.

3. *Conduct a valuation.* The feasibility study will rely on rough estimates
    of the value of the stock for the purpose of calculating the adequacy
    of cash and payroll. In public companies, of course, these estimates
    will be fairly accurate because they can be based on past price per-
    formance. In private companies, they will be more speculative. The
    next step for private companies (and some public companies as well)
    is a valuation. A company may want to have a preliminary valua-
    tion done first to see if the range of values produced is acceptable.
    A full valuation would follow if it is.

    Doing a valuation before implementing a plan is a critical step.
    If the value is too low, sellers may not be willing to sell. Or, the price
    of the shares may be too high for the company to afford. The valua-
    tion consultant will look at a variety of factors, including cash flow,
    profits, market conditions, assets, comparable company values,
    goodwill, and overall economic factors. A discount on value may be
    taken if the ESOP is buying less than 5% of the shares. The process
    is described in more detail later in this book.

4. *Hire an ESOP attorney.* If these first three steps prove positive, the
    plan can now be drafted and submitted to the IRS. You should care-
    fully evaluate your options and tell your attorney just how you want
    the ESOP to be set up. This could save you a considerable amount
    of money in consultation time. The IRS may take many months to

issue you a "letter of determination" on your plan, but you can go ahead and start making contributions before then. If the IRS rules unfavorably, which rarely happens, normally you simply need to amend your plan.

5. *Obtain funding for the plan.* There are several potential sources of funding. Obviously, the ESOP can borrow money. Banks are generally receptive to ESOP loans, but, as with any loan, it makes sense to shop around. Sellers or other private parties can also make loans, but do not qualify for the interest income exclusion. Larger ESOP transactions can also tap the bond market or borrow from insurance companies. Another source of funding is ongoing company contributions, outside of loan repayments. While ESOPs must, by law, invest primarily in employer securities, most ESOP experts believe they can temporarily invest primarily in other assets while building up a fund to buy out an owner. A third source is existing benefit plans. Pension plans are not a practical source of funding, but profit sharing plans are sometimes used. Profit sharing assets are simply transferred in part, or entirely, into an ESOP. Many ESOP companies do this, but it must be done cautiously. If employees are given no choice in the switch, trustees of the plan must be able to demonstrate that the investment in company stock was prudent; if they are given a choice, there could be a securities law issue. Finally, employees can contribute to the plan, most commonly by wage or benefit concessions. Most ESOPs do not require these, but they are necessary in some cases. Clearly, this is an issue that must be handled very carefully.

6. *Establish a process to operate the plan.* A trustee must be chosen to oversee the plan. In most private companies, this will be someone from inside the firm, but some private and most public companies hire an outside trustee. An ESOP committee will direct the trustee. In most companies, this is made up of management people, but many ESOP companies allow at least some nonmanagement representation. Finally, and most important, a process must be established to communicate how the plan works to employees and to get them more involved as owners. These issues are also addressed in more detail later in this book.

Freezing or Terminating an ESOP

Every year, perhaps 3% or 4% of all ESOPs are terminated; an unknown percentage are frozen, usually because the company wants to create a different kind of benefit plan, to recapture some of the ESOP's ownership, or, more rarely, has financial problems. Terminating or freezing a plan is a decision that can be made by the plan sponsor, but, in both cases, there are special considerations that must be taken into account.

Freezing an ESOP

When an ESOP is "frozen," no further contributions are made, and the participants are paid for their accounts under the normal rules of the plan as if it were still operating. The ESOP trust continues after the plan is frozen (also known as a wasting trust) with the assets remaining in the trust to be distributed under the provisions of the plan document. Freezing the plan may result in affected participants becoming fully vested if it results in a partial termination. Freezing a plan requires the company to continue to have annual valuations, submit reports to the government, follow top-heavy rules, and run the risk of being sued for plan improprieties.

The decision to freeze the ESOP is generally due to the burden of the company's ESOP repurchase obligation. If a company terminates an ESOP and distributes participants' account balances, the company must come up with the cash to fund the repurchase of the shares. If the company is not being sold, this is often a prohibitive cash requirement on the company. It is common to freeze the ESOP and merge the ESOP with another qualified plan of the employer, such as a 401(k) plan. Thus, there is only one plan with one participant's statement, allocation report, plan document, Form 5500, and audit by a CPA firm. The only additional cost would involve the cost of the annual valuation update.

Terminating an ESOP

A company has the right to terminate its ESOP at any time, although if the termination is not due to the sale of the company, going public, or financial difficulty, it could raise some concerns about the original intention of the plan and who it was designed to benefit. One circuit court ruling, however, has held that plan termination is not a fiduciary decision covered by ERISA, so the ability of plan participants to sue over a plan's termination under this statute is doubtful. It is not necessary to get Internal Revenue Service (IRS) approval to terminate a plan, but it is advisable.

When a plan is terminated, all participants become fully vested. The amounts allocated to participants are paid out directly or rolled over into a successor plan. The normal distribution rules apply; thus, payouts for the distribution can be made in equal installments with adequate security and interest over up to five years (more in the case of accounts worth over \$800,000 in 2002 dollars). Also, the distribution will generally be subject to the participant's consent (and spousal consent, if applicable). The amounts can be rolled over into a qualified successor plan, such as a 401(k) plan or profit sharing plan, or into an IRA, and employee taxes will be deferred. Otherwise, employees who receive the payouts will have to pay both income taxes and a 10% penalty (there are exceptions to the 10% penalty, such as distributions after age 59½).

In any termination there are fiduciary issues. Although the company has the right to terminate the plan, the ESOP fiduciaries must decide at what price and on what terms this may take place. Shareholders or corporate insiders have a clear conflict of interest if they or their employer are repurchasing shares or selling the company. Either an outside trustee should be appointed or, at the very least, qualified, independent advisors should be enlisted. A new valuation should be performed, one that might change some of the assumptions of the previous valuation (for example, if the buyer is obtaining control by buying ESOP-held shares, a control premium may now be appropriate).

If the ESOP loan is still outstanding when the plan is terminated, the proceeds from the sale of unallocated shares are then used to repay the remaining amount due on the ESOP loan. If that is not enough to repay the loan, the company makes up the difference. If it is more than enough, the "windfall" is allocated to employee accounts, either on the basis of the plan's usual allocation formula or according to the relative amounts each participant already has allocated. There is no consensus on the right way to do this.

Partial Terminations

A partial termination of an ESOP or other qualified plan occurs when a significant portion of the workforce is terminated (also known as a "vertical" partial termination) or otherwise loses its rights to benefits under the plan, such as the cessation of contributions or the tightening of vesting requirements (also known as a "horizontal" partial termination). What constitutes a partial termination is based on "facts and circumstances," not a precise guideline. Generally, however, a "vertical" partial termination is deemed to occur if 20% or more of the participants in the plan are laid off. Some employers voluntarily declare a partial termination for a smaller percentage of its workforce to make sure the affected employees are fully vested.

When a partial termination occurs, affected participants (but only affected participants) must become fully vested. The partial termination does not affect the timing or form of distributions.

Section 401(k) Plans As an Employee Ownership Vehicle

Section 401(k) plans allow employees to defer part of their pay on a pretax basis into an investment fund set up by the company. The company usually offers at least four alternative investment vehicles. Because the law requires that participation in the plans not be too heavily skewed towards more highly paid people, companies generally offer a partial match to encourage broad participation in these voluntary plans. This match can be in any investment vehicle the company chooses, including company stock. There is a limit of 25% of eligible pay that the company can contribute to the plan on a tax-deductible basis. This limit is reduced by other employer contributions to defined contribution plans.

While ESOPs have received the lion's share of attention as the vehicle of choice for employee ownership, 401(k) plans actually now hold almost as much company stock as ESOPs do. Most of the "company's own stock" investments in 401(k) plans are in larger companies. In companies with fewer than 200 employees, only 2% is in company stock; it is 8% in companies under 1,000 employees. This increases to 17% for companies with 1,000 to 5,000 people and 32.4% for companies over

5,000. These data also reveal how much of 401(k) assets are in larger companies in general. In companies with over 1,000 employees, a Hewitt Associates study found that 25% of employee contributions to 401(k) plans are in company stock, while about 70% of employer matches are in the form of company stock. Collectively, about 18% of 401(k) assets are in company stock, which, as of 2002, would be worth roughly $200 billion.

While these numbers add up to impressive absolute amounts, employees rarely own more than 10% of a company through a 401(k) plan. Moreover, our research at the NCEO has found few companies that provide stock in this way think of themselves as "employee ownership companies." Instead, companies simply see this as a convenient or financially favorable investment option.

The continued growth of 401(k) plans suggests, however, that they must be taken seriously as employee ownership vehicles. Over the next decade, if current trends continue, employees could own 20% or more of many large, public companies. While it is only speculation, we think that when a certain percentage of ownership is reached, corporate management may start realizing that it would be to its advantage to start thinking of itself as a substantially employee-owned company, just as employees will start realizing how much their retirement benefits depend on company performance.

There are several factors that favor the use of a 401(k) plan as a vehicle for employee ownership in public companies. From the company's perspective, its own stock may be one of the most cost-effective means of matching employee contributions. If there are existing treasury shares or the company prints new shares, contributing them to the 401(k) plan may impose no immediate cash cost on the company; in fact, it would provide a tax deduction. Other shareholders would suffer a dilution, of course. If the company has to buy shares to fund the match, at least the dollars being used are invested in itself rather than other investments. From the employee standpoint, company stock is the investment the employee knows best, and so it may be attractive to people who either do not want to spend the time to learn about alternatives or have a strong belief in their own company. Balanced against these advantages, of course, must be an appreciation on both the part of the employee and the company that a failure to diversify a retirement portfolio is very risky.

For closely held companies, 401(k) plans are less appealing, although very appropriate in some cases. If employees are given an option to buy company stock, this can often trigger securities law issues most private companies want to avoid. Employer matches make more sense, but require the company to either dilute ownership or reacquire shares from selling shareholders. In many closely held businesses, the first option (employee purchases) may be undesirable for control reasons and the second (employer matches) may be undesirable because there may not be sellers. Moreover, the 401(k) approach does not provide the "rollover" tax benefit that selling to an ESOP does, and the maximum amount that can be contributed is a function of how much employees put into savings. That will limit how much an employer can actually buy from a seller through a 401(k) plan to a fraction of what the ESOP can buy.

401(k) contributions cannot be leveraged either, so a sale of company stock would have to proceed slowly in annual increments. For example, if a company can get 60% of its workforce to participate in a 401(k) plan, and they put up 5% of pay (a reasonable but fairly high amount in practice), the company might match this on a dollar-for-dollar basis, but this would still only come to perhaps 4% of payroll (assuming 401(k) participants tend to be higher paid than nonparticipants).

Despite these limitations, 401(k) plans, and their new, simpler cousins, SIMPLE plans (plans for employers under 100 employees that are much like 401(k) plans but with stricter rules and easier administration), are attractive as ownership vehicles in cases where a company simply wants employees to become owners, but has no need to buy out owners or use the borrowing features of an ESOP. A company can simply match employee deferrals with company stock or make a straight percentage of pay contribution to all eligible employees in the form of company stock.

Section 401(k) plans and ESOPs can also be combined, with the ESOP contribution being used as the 401(k) match. This can work on either a nonleveraged or leveraged basis. In the nonleveraged case, the company simply characterizes its match as an ESOP. That adds some set-up and administrative costs, but allows the company to reap the additional tax benefits of an ESOP, such as the 1042 rollover. In a leveraged ESOP, the company estimates how much it will need to match employee contributions each year, then borrows an amount of money such that the loan repayment will be close to that amount. If it is not as much as the promised matching amount, the company can either just define that as its match anyway, make up the difference with additional shares or cash (if the loan payment is lower), or pay the loan faster. If the amount is larger, the employees get a windfall. Combination plans must meet complex rules for testing to determine if they discriminate too heavily in favor of more highly paid people.

Employee Ownership and Employee Motivation

During the early 1980s, we at the NCEO conducted an exhaustive investigation of how employees react to being owners. We surveyed over 3,500 employee owners in 45 companies. We looked at hundreds of factors in an effort to determine whether it mattered to employees that they had stock in their company, and if so, when.

The results were very clear. Employees did like being owners. The more shares they owned, the more committed they were to their company, the more satisfied they were with their jobs, and the less likely they were to leave. Naturally, some employees in some companies liked being owners more than others. Individual employee response to ownership was primarily a response to how much stock they got each year. After that, employees responded more favorably if they had ample opportunities to participate in decisions affecting their jobs, worked in companies whose management really believed in the concept of ownership and not just the tax breaks, and were provided regular information about how the ownership plan operated.

By contrast, the size of the company, the line of business, demographic characteristics of the employees, seniority, job classification, presence or absence of voting rights or board membership, percentage of the company owned by employees (as opposed to the size of the annual contribution), and many other factors did not have any impact. Employees looked at the employee ownership plan and asked "how much money will I get from this?" and "am I really treated like an owner?" If they liked the answers to these questions, they liked being an owner.

Employee Ownership and Corporate Performance

In 2000, Douglas Kruse and Joseph Blasi of Rutgers University analyzed all the ESOPs set up between 1988 and 1994 for which data were available. They then matched these companies to comparable non-ESOP companies and looked at the sales and employment data for the paired companies for three years before a company set up an ESOP to the period three years after. They found that when they indexed out for the performance of the competitor companies, the ESOP companies grew 2.3% to 2.4% faster after setting up their plan than would have been expected otherwise. That seemed to give strong evidence that ESOPs do make a significant and positive contribution to corporate performance.

Impressive as these findings were, however, they did not indicate what it was about employee ownership that caused the improved performance or whether the improved performance was accounted for by just a subset of ESOP companies with particular characteristics. Other research, however, suggests that it is the combination of employee ownership and employee involvement that really makes the difference.

Knowing the answer to whether employee ownership motivates employees may seem to provide the answer to whether ownership improves corporate performance. Not so. In most companies, labor costs are under 30% to 40% of total costs. Motivation on its own, presumably, makes employees work harder. We often ask managers how much more work they think they could hope to get from more motivated employees, based on an eight-hour day. Fifteen minutes is a typical response. That comes to just 3% more time. Three percent times even a high estimate of 40% for labor costs results in just a 1.2% savings, assuming everyone will be more motivated, which is, of course, far from true.

While a 1% improvement can be a lot of money, it is not what distinguishes the really successful companies from the mediocre ones. The star performers are those that react to their environment in creative, innovative ways, providing better value to their customers than competitors. How is that achieved? Through processing information and acting on it intelligently. In most companies, information gathering is limited to a group of managers. The generation of ideas is similarly limited. So is decision-making. The assumption is that only these people have the talent, and perhaps motivation, to carry out these tasks.

In fact, no one has more daily contact with customers than employees, at least in most companies. No one is closer to the day-to-day process of making the product or providing the service than the employees. And employees often do have useful ideas they could share with management.

Thus, for a company to use employee ownership effectively, it needs to do more than motivate people to work harder at what, after all, may not be the most efficient or effective thing to do. Instead, it must enlist employee ideas and information to find the best ways to do the most important things. To do that, companies need to get employees involved. Managers should seek their opinions. Employee task forces, ad hoc and permanent, should be established to solve problems. Quality circles and employee involvement teams can be set up. Individual jobs can be enhanced and supervision limited. Suggestion systems can be implemented. This all may seem like common sense, and it is. It is not very common practice in most companies, however.

Data indicate that it *is* becoming common in employee ownership companies. In a 1987 General Accounting Office report, about one-third of all ESOP companies had some degree of employee participation. By 1993, a study of Ohio companies by the Northeast Ohio Employee Ownership Center and Kent State University found that about 60% of the companies now had active employee involvement programs, such as autonomous work teams, total quality management, or similar programs. The incidence of participation roughly doubled after the initiation of an ownership plan. These participative companies, the GAO reported, showed a strong improvement in productivity when they combined their ESOPs with participative management practices.

In a study by the National Center for Employee Ownership published in the September/October 1987 *Harvard Business Review*, we found that participative ESOP companies grew 8% to 11% faster with their plans than they would have without them. In both the NCEO and GAO studies, no other factors had any influence on the relationship between ownership and performance. Three other recent studies confirmed both the direction and magnitude of these findings. Only participation can translate the motivation of ownership into the reality of a fatter bottom line. Participation is not enough on its own, either, as hundreds of studies have shown. One reason is that few participation programs last more than five years in conventional companies. By contrast, over the last decade we have not found a single ESOP company that has dropped its program.

The structure of participation varies from company to company, but basically boils down to employees forming groups to share information, generate ideas, and make recommendations.

At United Airlines, for instance, employee task teams were formed soon after the employees purchased the company. Over the ensuing two years, the teams took apart every aspect of the business, making recommendations for often substantial changes. The teams were appointed to include a broad cross section of employees, but anyone could volunteer to join one. The ideas helped generate hundreds of millions of dollars in cost savings and new revenues. Ironically, when the teams completed their work, management backed away from the idea of participation, causing the airline some well-reported difficulties in the years that followed. The ESOP is now frozen, and both most managers and most employees feel that it was not a success. United shows clearly that just setting up an ESOP, and even starting off in the right direction, is not enough. Companies must commit to a long-term ownership culture program.

Stone Construction Equipment Company in Honoeye, New York, is a good example. It set up an ESOP in the late 1970s was having little impact. Then the company hired a new president, Bob Fien, who started a participative management program. Eventually, all employees were trained in "just-in-time" management and organized into work cells that schedule and control their own work flow and have considerable input into the design and organization of their jobs. Stone had been limping along and had developed a reputation for poor quality; by 1991, the company had made so much progress *Industry Week* named it one of America's top 10 manufacturers.

At Springfield ReManufacturing in Springfield, Missouri, employee owners are taught to read detailed financial and production data. Meeting in work groups, they go over the numbers and figure out ways to improve them. Employees are sometimes given 90-page financial statements to digest. Springfield's stock went from 10 cents a share when it started its ESOP in 1983 to $21 in 1994. Employment increased over 500%.

Other approaches include employee advisory committees to management, eliminating levels of supervision while giving non-management employees more authority, meetings between management and randomly selected groups of employees, suggestion boxes, and anything else companies can imagine to get people involved.

This "high-involvement" management style has, of course, become conventional wisdom, if still unconventional practice, at many companies. Is ownership really essential to make it work? There are no conclusive data on this, but there is good reason to believe that ownership, if not essential, is at least highly desirable. First, ownership is a cumulative benefit. Each additional year, an employee has more and more at stake in how well the company performs. It is not unusual in mature plans for the appreciation in share value and employer contributions to add up to 30% to 50% or more of pay in a year. In profit sharing or gainsharing, both of which are paid periodically and almost always amount to a small portion of total compensation, the benefit always remains relatively minor. Second, ownership has a stronger emotive appeal. People may be very proud to say they are an owner; few would brag to friends they are a profit-sharer. Finally, only ownership encourages people to think about all aspects of a business, not just short term profits or some efficiency measure. This is especially important in companies moving towards open-book management systems.

Conclusion

The continued growth of employee ownership reflects, above all, a changing view of the role of employees in the workplace. To be sure, for some time companies have been saying that "people are our most important resource." This was little more than rhetoric, however, for all but a handful of companies. Investors, capital, technology, and, above all, top management, were really seen as the keys to the company's future. Employees would be laid off or have their compensation limited before these other assets were harmed. Increasingly, however, companies are coming to the view that attracting and retaining good people at all levels, then giving them the authority to make more decisions about more things, is essential to being an effective competitor. In large part, this is a function of technology. The vast amounts of information, and the speed with which it can be processed, leaves companies with little choice but to get more people involved in more things. As people are asked to take more responsibility for the company, it simply makes sense for them to be rewarded accordingly.

CHAPTER 2

Using an ESOP for Business Continuity

Corey Rosen

One of the most difficult problems for small business owners is finding a way to turn their equity in a business into cash for retirement or other purposes. The decision to sell is more than an economic one, however. After putting years into a business, an owner develops a strong feeling of identity with the company. At the same time, the owner often has a sense of loyalty to the employees and would like to see them have a continuing role in the company.

For some business owners, the answer to these problems will be to turn over the company to an heir. Others may find a buyer willing to offer an adequate price or have managers or partners interested in buying the company. But many owners do not have heirs interested in the business, and outside buyers are not easy to find. Even if they can be found, they may want to buy the company for its customer lists, technology, or facilities, or may just want to put a competitor out of business. They may have little interest in keeping key employees or even any employees, and often will not continue the corporate identity the owner has worked so hard to build. Owners hoping to gain liquidity may be forced to sell the entire company, even though they may have partners still interested in the business, may want to keep partial ownership themselves, or hope to keep some continuing employment role in the company. Selling to a few key employees can be an option, but only if these employees have substantial capital of their own and are willing to take considerable financial risks in order to buy the business.

Faced with these problems, some owners simply hope that some solution will present itself "later down the road." Of course, it rarely does, and the business ends up in an estate and is sold under fire-sale circumstances to pay taxes. Others end up liquidating the firm, or having the firm redeem their shares gradually. Redemption can solve some problems, but the funds used to buy the shares are not deductible to the company, so this becomes a costly way to plan for retirement.

Fortunately, the tax laws provide an alternative that a great many business owners will find very attractive: selling to the employees through an ESOP. For the owner of a C corporaiton, proceeds on the gain made from the sale to the ESOP can be tax-deferred by reinvesting in the securities of other domestic companies. If these securities are not sold prior to the owner's death, no capital gains tax is ever due. For the company, the owner's shares are bought in tax-deductible dollars, either from company contributions or plan borrowings. The sale can be all at once or gradual, for as little or as much of the stock as desired. For the employees, no contributions are required to purchase the owner's shares. The owner can stay with the business in whatever capacity is desired.

Using an ESOP to Transfer Ownership

The simplest way to use an ESOP to transfer ownership is to have the company make tax-deductible cash contributions to the ESOP trust, which the trust then uses to gradually purchase the owner's shares.

Alternatively, the owner can have the ESOP borrow the funds needed to buy the shares. In this way, larger amounts of stock can be purchased all at once, up to 100% of the equity. Normally, the bank will loan to the company, which then reloans to the ESOP, not necessarily on the same terms. In some cases, such as when the total debt would exceed current book value, the bank may also want a personal guarantee, or may be willing to loan only part of the total sought. In that case, the ESOP would buy part of the shares now, and part after some of the debt has been paid. If a commercial lender cannot be found, the owner can take back a note. In this scenario, the rollover would apply only to what is reinvested in the first year, however. The entire amount of the sale could only be reinvested, therefore, if the seller has other funds available. However the money is obtained, the price is set by an independent appraiser, as discussed below.

If the company is a C corporation, once the ESOP owns 30% of the company's shares, if the owner reinvests the gains in the securities of other U.S. companies (other than real estate trusts, mutual funds, and other passive investments) within 12 months after or three months before the sale, no taxes are due until the replacement securities are sold. If the owner buys income-yielding securities and lives on the proceeds, giving them to an estate at death, no capital gains tax is due. If part of the securities are sold, tax is due only on a prorated basis. (This tax incentive is not available for S corporation owners.)

Compare the ESOP buyout to two other common methods of selling an owner's shares: redemption or sale to another firm. Under a redemption, the company gradually repurchases the shares of an owner. Corporate funds used to do this are not deductible. Moreover, the owner must pay ordinary income tax on the gain. In a sale to a C corporation ESOP, the money made is considered a capital gain, not ordinary income, and taxes can be deferred. Or consider the second alternative, selling to another company or individual. In a cash sale, taxes would be due immediately. If the sale is for an exchange of stock in the acquiring company, taxes can be deferred until the new stock is sold, but 80% of the company must be sold all at once and the owner ends up with an undiversified investment for retirement.

In short, Congress has made a point of making selling to an ESOP the most tax-favored way of providing for business continuity. It is also among the most flexible, allowing the owner to sell out as quickly or slowly as desired. The owner is assured of a fair price for the stock and has the knowledge that the company will continue as an independent business in the hands of the employees.

Estate Considerations

In private companies, ESOPs can also help in estate planning. For many people, one of the most important of these aspects is that the ESOP provides a market for shares. After the death of a principal owner, businesses may often be liquidated to pay taxes. With an ESOP, the company can use tax-deductible dollars to buy out the estate's interest in an orderly manner. Ongoing prior valuations will have established a fair price, avoiding potential legal battles.

ESOPs also can be used for charitable purposes. An owner can contribute shares of company stock to a charity, university, or other qualified beneficiary, deducting the value of the contribution. The beneficiary then sells the shares to the ESOP. The owner gets a deduction, the beneficiary gets cash, and the employees get stock.

Valuing the Shares

The price the ESOP will pay for the shares, as well as any other purchases, must be determined at least annually by an outside, independent appraiser. The appraiser's valuation will be based on several factors. Most appraisers try first to find comparable public companies and use their price/earnings ratio, price/assets ratio, and other guides for setting a price. Discounted cash flow, book value, the company's reputation, future market considerations, and other factors will be considered as well. The appraiser will try, as much as possible, to determine how much the business would be worth if there were a market for it.

Many owners wonder why they cannot just use book value. One reason is that the law specifically requires regular valuations. Aside from that, book value makes no adjustments for changing market conditions, the company's reputation, expected cash flow, and other key issues that can have a dramatic impact on value.

An ESOP also adds a number of special considerations. If it is buying less than a majority of the stock, for instance, there may be a "lack of control" discount of about 10% to 40%. Some appraisers will ignore this if there is a specific plan for the ESOP to acquire a majority interest, whether or not the shares will be voted on all issues. There is also a discount in private firms for lack of marketability. Some appraisers argue that an ESOP provides a market, with a legal obligation to repurchase the shares of its beneficiaries. They may reduce this discount accordingly. Third, if the company uses cash to buy out an owner or borrow money through the ESOP, the value of the company after the ESOP transaction will be reduced, at least in the short run. That could affect other owners, or the selling owner's interest in his or her remaining shares.

Different valuation experts view each of these issues differently, so it is best to discuss them in advance.

Who Will Run the Company?

For most owners, the key issue is the price the ESOP will pay. Not far behind, however, is concern about possibly losing control of the company before they actually leave. In most cases, this is not a problem. The owner of the company makes the ESOP decision and sets up the plan. The plan can be terminated at any time, and the amount contributed each year is discretionary, except for amounts contributed to repaying a loan. The ESOP is governed by a committee, which can be appointed by management or elected by the employees (or a combination). The committee appoints a trustee, usually from a bank trust department or a manager. The trustee administers the plan and technically votes the shares. In fact, the trustee only votes the shares at either the direction of the committee or the employees, where votes are voluntarily passed through. If the ESOP borrows money, shares are held in a suspense account and released to employee accounts only as the loan is repaid. Suspense account shares are voted by the trustee at the direction of the committee. So the owner can control voting for the board on all matters with the exception of the limited number of legally required pass-through issues.

When employees do vote, they tend to be very conservative shareholders and almost invariably support management, including electing management to the board.

This means that the selling owner can choose to stay with the company in whatever capacity seems appropriate, and many owners do retain an active role.

Sources of Capital

As mentioned earlier, ESOPs can use corporate cash contributions, commercial loans, or loans from the owner to buy shares. There are four other potential sources of capital:

1. *Managers may buy shares on their own.* The ESOP can own as much or as little of the company as desired, and in some cases, key people may want to buy more of the company than their ESOP allocation would provide them. These additional shares are bought in the traditional way, outside the ESOP. The equity these purchases provide may be very important in securing a loan.

2. *Employees may be willing to take lower wages or benefits in return for the ESOP.* Almost all ESOPs require no employee concessions, but in some special cases, concessions may be needed to assure the cash flow to buy out an owner. By having employees take lower wages, rather than buy stock directly, employees avoid having to use after-tax dollars on their purchase and both employees and the company avoid paying employment taxes on the foregone wages.

3. *Part or all of a profit sharing or 401(k) plan's assets can be rolled into the ESOP.* Many companies considering an ESOP have one of these plans, sometimes with substantial assets. Plan assets contributed by the company can be transferred into the ESOP to buy shares, but only under certain conditions. If all or part of the assets are put into the ESOP, with no provisions for allowing employees to choose whether to move their assets individually, the trustee of the ESOP must be able to demonstrate, at any future point, that the transfer was prudent. For instance, if a profit sharing plan were earning a competitive rate of return, but the shares in the ESOP decline in value, the employees could sue the trustee and the company. This is unlikely unless there is both a dramatic difference in the performance of the two plans and reason to believe that those conducting the transaction should have known or did know that investing in company shares would not be a sound decision. Although suits along these lines have been rare, this approach to raising capital should be approached cautiously. Most experts say the best approach is to move under 30% of profit sharing assets into the ESOP.

   Alternatively, the employees can be given an individual choice about having their account balances transferred. This helps avoid the fiduciary problems, but it could require a securities law registration if an exemption is not available and, in any event, will require extensive (and often costly) financial disclosure documentation to all employees.

   If money that employees have deferred into a 401(k) plan is used, employees must be able to decide whether and how much of their assets should be moved into company stock in the ESOP. All relevant securities laws would need to be complied with. Advisors generally urge clients not to use these funds for an ESOP.

4. As noted earlier, the owner can make a loan directly or guarantee a loan personally. All transactions with an ESOP, however, must be made on an arm's length or equivalent basis.

Special Rules When Using the Rollover Treatment

If gains are reinvested to defer taxation (remember, this is only possible with C corporation ESOPs), there are some special rules to consider. First, they can only be invested in the securities (stocks, bonds, etc.) of domestic corporations earning less than 25% of their income from the passive management of assets. Generally, mutual finds, investment trusts, and any type of government securities are not allowable.

Second, neither the sellers, their direct family members, nor any 25% shareholders can, if they are also employees, participate in the allocation of shares to the ESOP resulting from the sale of stock for which tax deferral treatment is selected. In some businesses, this may have a more negative financial impact on those concerned than not taking the deferral. Disqualified people can, however, get allocations from sources other than rolled-over shares.

Third, the rollover cannot be taken unless the stock sold to the ESOP has been held by the seller for at least three years before the sale.

Fourth, for sales on the installment basis, there may be some limits on how much can be reinvested that will qualify for rollover treatment. The entire amount of the sale, or some portion of it, can be rolled over into qualified replacement property, but sellers must make a qualifying investment within 12 months of the initiation of the sale. Money from other savings can be used for this purpose. If sellers do not have these funds to invest, then they can only roll over the payments made in the first 12 months. For instance, on a $1 million sale with $200,000 in payments the first year, a seller could roll over $1 million by investing the $200,000 plus $800,000 from other sources of income. If the seller does not have the income to invest, then only the $200,000 would qualify. One increasingly popular way to deal with this is for the seller to buy a very long-term qualifying replacement property bond (called an "ESOP note"), using money borrowed from a bank. The bond acts as collateral on the loan. Then the seller takes a note from the ESOP, and uses the repayment on the note to pay off the loan to buy the bond. This transaction requires the advice of people specialized in this kind of transaction.

Fifth, if the ESOP's holdings fall below 30% in the three years after the rollover was elected, there will be a 10% excise tax imposed on sale proceeds. This rule does not apply to additional shares sold by the company to investors or if the shortfall is the result of the company buying and retiring shares from departing employees. Most commonly, it would apply if the company issues new shares to additional holders (such as giving new shares to a family member).

Making the Decision

All of this may sound appealing, but it is not feasible for every company. Several factors must, at a minimum, be present:

1. *The company is making enough money to buy out an owner.* The company must be generating enough cash to buy the shares, conduct its normal business, and make necessary reinvestments. How much will be needed depends on the price over the life of the buyout. The company will need a business plan to determine this.

2. *Payroll must be adequate to cover the purchase.* The company can generally only deduct up to 25% of the payroll of plan participants to cover the principal portion of an ESOP loan. Payroll includes only those people in the ESOP. If sellers are rolling over their gains from the sale of stock, certain family members or key employees may be excluded from receiving stock allocations from the ESOP, and their salaries would not be counted as a result. Moreover, company (but not employee) contributions to profit sharing, stock bonus, pension, 401(k), and similar plans also will reduce the total amount the company can contribute to the ESOP. In addition, no one employee can receive more than 100% of pay in any one year from company and employee contributions to these plans, or (in 2002 dollars) $40,000, whichever is less.

   If payroll is not adequate to cover the costs of repurchasing shares, the company may be able to pay dividends on the ESOP shares in order to help repay the loan. Dividends would not count towards the 25% limit. Issuing high dividend-paying convertible preferred stock to the ESOP may also help to overcome the 25% rule. The terms of the loan from the ESOP to the company could also be stretched out. For instance, if the company has a seven-year loan from the bank that would require a 35% annual contribution to the ESOP to cover the principal portion of the loan, stretching out the term of the company-to-ESOP loan to, say 11 years, could be lower the contribution levels to 25% of pay or less. The extension of the loan terms must be done to benefit plan participants, however. This clearly would—there would be no ESOP otherwise. Stretching out the internal loan so that repayment levels were significantly below 25%, however, would be harder (if not necessarily impossible) to justify.

3. *If the company is borrowing to buy the shares, its existing debt must not prevent it from taking out an adequate loan.* Similarly, the company must not have bonding covenants or other agreements that prohibit it from taking on additional debt.

4. *If the seller wants to take the tax-deferred rollover, the company must be a regular C corporation or convert from S to C status.* S corporations can establish ESOPs, but their owners cannot take advantage of the tax-deferred rollover described above. Additionally, in S corporations, interest paid on an ESOP loan counts towards these contribution limits, and dividends paid to the ESOP or to ESOP participants are not deductible. For all these reasons, ESOPs are used in S corporations mostly as a benefit plan, not a business continuity or financing tool. Many S corporations find it worth converting to C status, however. The costs of such a conversion are minimal.

5. *Special considerations do not require the ESOP to pay less than an outside buyer would.* An ESOP will pay the appraised fair market value based on a variety of factors, but sometimes an outside buyer can pay more for a company if it has a particular fit that creates synergies that go beyond what the company is worth on its own.

6. *Management continuity is provided.* Banks, suppliers, and customers will all want to be persuaded that the company can continue to operate successfully. It is essential that people be trained to take the place of departing owners to assure a smooth transition.

7. *Legal costs are not so high that the deal is impractical.* The first-year costs of an ESOP—feasibility studies, valuation, plan design, administration, and possibly investment banking services in larger deals—start at a bare minimum of $20,000 and can be much higher. Ongoing costs will be one-third to one-half of these start-up fees.

Conclusion

For many owners of closely held companies, an ESOP is an ideal solution. For others, it simply will not work. To make a decision, create an initial business plan, factoring in legal costs, the costs to buy the shares, and the company's cash flow. If that looks encouraging, talk to an accountant about your figures. If things still look promising, have a valuation done. Your valuation specialist will tell you how much your stock is worth and should also give you a more detailed idea about the practicality of selling these shares. If things still look good, hire a qualified ESOP attorney to draft your plan. As you consider an ESOP, find some other ESOP company executives to talk to, attend an ESOP meeting or two, and finalize your plans with all the key players.

CHAPTER 3

ESOPs in S Corporations

Corey Rosen

In 1996, Congress allowed ESOPs and other employee benefit trusts to own stock in an S corporation, effective January 1, 1998. In 1997, Congress amended the law (also effective January 1, 1998) to correct technical flaws in the first law. The 1997 law also provides S corporations sponsoring ESOPs with significant tax benefits, while excluding them from other tax benefits available to C corporation ESOPs. In 2001, in the Economic Growth and Tax Relief Reconciliation Act created new rules to prevent abuses of the new law. It also increased contribution limits for S corporation ESOPs. The effect of these laws can be summarized as follows:

1. Profits attributable to ESOP ownership of S corporation stock are exempt from federal income tax. Thus, a 100% ESOP S corporation becomes the only form of corporate structure Congress intentionally exempted from federal income tax.

2. Sellers to ESOPs in S corporation ESOPs cannot qualify for the Section 1042 deferral of capital gains taxes available to qualifying sellers to ESOPs in C corporations.

3. Interest paid on ESOP loans in S corporation ESOPs counts toward the maximum amount that can be contributed to the plan, whereas it generally does not in C corporation ESOPs.

4. S corporations cannot deduct dividends (or "distributions," as they are more properly called in S corporations and will be referred to as here) used to repay an ESOP loan, that are passed through to par-

ticipants, or that participants reinvest in company stock. If they use distributions to repay a loan, the IRS has stated in a private letter ruling that they can only use distributions on unallocated shares (shares not yet paid for), whereas in C corporations dividends on all ESOP shares can be used to repay a loan.

5. S corporation ESOPs designed primarily to benefit one person or a small number of people, including those intended solely or principally to benefit management or existing corporate owners, will potentially be subject to severe tax penalties.

S Corporations and ESOPs: The Evolution of the Law

S corporations are forms of business ownership in which the corporation does not pay tax on its earnings. Instead, owners of the S corporation pay tax on their proportionate share of the company's earnings at their own individual tax rates. S corporations often pay a distribution to these owners equal to the amount of tax they owe. When owners of an S corporation sell their ownership interest, they pay capital gains taxes on the gain. Their basis is increased by allocations of earnings on which they have paid taxes. S corporations allow owners to avoid the double taxation on corporate earnings that must be paid in C corporations (the company pays taxes on profits; the owners pay taxes when the profits are distributed). Top C corporation tax rates are currently (2002) somewhat lower than top individual rates, however. S corporations can only have one class of stock and no more than 75 owners.

Until 1998, S corporations could not have an ESOP that owned stock in the company, because ESOPs are non-profit trusts, which could not own stock in an S corporation because the trust would not pay tax, thus allowing a portion of the earnings to go untaxed. In 1997, Congress exempted ESOPs (and, among trusts that can be owners, only ESOPs) from the unrelated business income tax (UBIT). If an ESOP owns 30% of the company, for instance, 30% of the earnings would go untaxed. Theoretically, ESOP participants pay this tax when their shares are distributed to them (their basis in the shares would be lower than that of other owners who had paid tax, hence their taxable gain would be higher), but participants have the option of rolling their distributions into an IRA and deferring tax further.

The 1997 law also allows S corporations to require that departing employees take their distributions in the form of cash rather than stock, thus avoiding the potential disqualification that could occur if an employee put the stock into an IRA, a disqualified S corporation owner. The law also made some technical changes to assure that ESOPs in S corporations will not run afoul of "prohibited transaction" rules under the Employee Retirement Income Security Act (ERISA).

Although these changes made ESOPs both possible and attractive in S corporations, S corporation ESOPs do not have all the same tax benefits that a C corporation ESOP has. Under Internal Revenue Code Section 1042, owners selling to an ESOP in a closely held C corporation can defer taxation on any gain they report from the sale of stock to an ESOP owning 30% or more of the company's shares; S corporation owners cannot. C corporations sponsoring ESOPs can deduct up to 25% of the eligible pay of ESOP participants to repay the principal on an ESOP loan, and interest payments on the loan do not count toward these limits. Eligible pay excludes pay over $200,000 per year (in 2002; this number is adjusted upward annually), pay of employees not in the plan, and any other pay the plan document defines as ineligible. In S corporations, however, interest payments are included in the 25% limit, thus lowering the amount that can be contributed.

In both S and C corporations, corporate contributions to an ESOP are added to corporate contributions to other retirement plans to test for compliance with the 25% of eligible pay limit on corporate contributions. Also, no one can have more than $40,000 in contributions to retirement plans, including company and employee contributions, added to their account in any one year. The combination of contributions also cannot exceed 100% of any individual's annual pay.

C corporation ESOPs also can deduct dividends used to repay an ESOP loan, dividends that are passed directly through to participants, or dividends participants voluntarily reinvest in company stock in the ESOP. S corporations technically do not pay dividends. Instead, they make distributions of earnings to shareholders. While these may be functionally comparable to dividends in C corporations, they are not technically the same and are not considered dividends for the purposes of tax deductions. S corporations that are 100% owned by an ESOP, of course, do not need to be concerned about deductibility. They don't pay federal income tax anyway. But for less-than-100% ESOPs in S corporations, the non-deductibility of dividends could increase taxes for other shareholders. As noted earlier, another difference is that distributions on unallocated shares in an ESOP trust can be used to repay an ESOP loan, but distributions on allocated shares cannot.

Issues in Deciding on Whether to Use an S or C Structure

For S corporation owners considering setting up an ESOP, the ability to avoid taxation on the ESOP's share of earnings is a powerful tax incentive. Where the goal of the ESOP is simply to provide a benefit to employees, there may be no reason to convert to C status. However, in a number of situations, there are special considerations.

Where the ESOP Is Being Used to Buy Out an Owner

Normally, if an owner wants to sell, an S corporation will first be converted to a C so the seller can defer gain on the sale. There are several scenarios, however, where owners of an S corporation may not want to do this:

1. *The seller is not the only owner.* While the seller benefits from the conversion to C status, the other owners now find any of their earnings that would have been sheltered from the corporate level tax no longer are. If the sale does not create enough deductions to reduce the corporate level tax low enough to satisfy these owners, they may not want to convert. Note, however, that the other owners may not face this problem if the C corporation ESOP creates enough debt or contribution obligations to reduce or eliminate the corporate-level tax. Also, earnings that would have been paid out to the owner in a S corporation could be paid out as compensation to those owners in a C corporation, creating almost as advantageous a tax situation because the corporation could deduct the compensation (note, however, that the compensation cannot be unreasonable, as defined by

the IRS, and that it will, unlike distributed earnings in the S corporation, be subject to payroll tax).

2. *There are large amounts of undistributed earnings.* When the conversion to C status takes place, any earnings that have not yet been contributed to the owners must be distributed in one year or they are taxable to the owners (meaning they will be taxed twice, since the owners have already paid tax on them before). If the company does not have the cash to do this, it could borrow money, but the ESOP may itself require too much cash to make this payout practical.

3. *Sellers plan to sell the company in an asset sale.* In an S corporation, the sale of the company's assets trigger only a single tax at the individual level; in a C corporation, the sale would be taxed at both the corporate and individual level, as income to the company and as capital gains to the individuals. The amount of the corporate tax would depend in part on the depreciation taken on the assets.

4. *The S corporation is creating losses the owners want flowed through to them.* In some situations, a company may be making heavy investments, often in real property or other hard assets, that create paper losses. These losses can be flowed through to the owners, who can deduct them at a marginally higher rate than can the company. In some scenarios, this may be desirable.

5. *The seller's basis is already very high because of taxes paid on previously undistributed earnings.* In this case, the "rollover" provision may not make much difference.

6. *There are multiple classes of stock, and it is important for the company or the ESOP to retain this feature.* For instance, if the ESOP has convertible preferred shares, changing to an S corporation would require they be converted to common shares. In some cases, this may not be practical. There is also a fiduciary issue for the conversion (whether it is in the interest of the ESOP participants as shareholders to convert) that could affect this transaction.

Cash Flow Considerations in Less Than 100% ESOPs

Where a company is 100% owned by an ESOP, conversion to an S is often a foregone conclusion. Why pay taxes when you don't have to? Barring special issues relating to converting from an S to a C, converting in 100% ownership situations is the norm. But where the ESOP owns less than 100% of the stock, the considerations are more complex.

Most S corporations make distributions to their shareholders in amounts at least large enough to cover their tax obligations. Because S corporations can have only one class of stock, if distributions are paid they must be paid to the ESOP as well. Because the ESOP does not pay taxes, the distributions it receives can create a pool of cash that can be used to buy additional shares or pay off a loan. In some scenarios we at the NCEO have seen, the distributions on the ESOP shares would be more than enough to pay for future planned share acquisitions. Any leftover distributions could be used to fund repurchase obligations. The distributions could also be used to buy more stock in the company. This would dilute the existing owners' percentage of ownership, but not their value (because an equivalent amount of cash had been brought back into the company). The company would now have additional cash.

Where the ESOP owns less than 100% of the stock, special attention must be paid to cash flow issues. Assume the ESOP owns 50%, for instance, and the company converts to an S corporation. Also assume the company makes distributions to shareholders in amounts at least sufficient to cover their taxes. Assume earnings of $1 million and that the personal tax rate of the owners is 40%. The company thus pays a distribution of $200,000 to the owners and $200,000 to the ESOP. Total retained earnings are now $600,000. If the company stayed a C corporation, and paid 38% state and federal tax on the $1 million earnings, it would have $620 million in retained earnings. The payout to owners, however, will increase their basis and thus reduce their long-term capital gains obligation. If owners in this scenario did not want to pay out earnings, but preferred to retain them for corporate reinvestment, or did not want the additional $200,000 going to the ESOP, converting would not make sense.

Issues for C Corporations with ESOPs Converting to S Status

Many C corporations with ESOPs are considering switching to S status. Especially where the ESOP owns a substantial part of the company's stock, this can provide a substantial tax benefit, even reducing taxes to zero where the ESOP owns 100% of the shares. Indeed, it is arguably a duty of ESOP fiduciaries to consider such a switch. Several issues must be kept in mind, however:

- The election requires the consent of all shareholders.

- An S corporation can only have 75 shareholders (the ESOP counts as one). S corporations can only have one class of stock, with the one exception that they can have voting and nonvoting common shares. Some C corporation ESOPs use convertible preferred or super-common stock for various reasons. These may or may not be sufficiently compelling issues to warrant remaining a C corporation.

- On conversion, S corporations using last in, first out (LIFO) accounting are subject to a LIFO recapture tax. This could be substantial in some cases, especially in capital-intensive businesses. If a company uses LIFO accounting procedures, there is an immediate recapture over four years of any excess inventory (not assets) with LIFO over what would have been the case with FIFO (first in, first out).

- For a 10-year period after conversion, if the company sells any asset it held on the day of its S corporation election, it will have to pay "built-in gains" tax on that sale. This tax is in addition to taxes paid by shareholders.

- In S corporations, some fringe benefits paid to 2% or more owners are taxable.

- Net operating losses incurred as a C corporation are suspended while the company remains an S corporation. These losses may be applied against LIFO or built-in gains taxes, however.

- State laws vary, and some states may not track federal laws. In California, for instance, ESOPs are subject to state unrelated business income tax.

- If there may be a desire or need to switch back to C status, remember that there is a fiduciary issue over whether the switch back to C would require the ESOP to get something back in return for what it has given up as an S corporation owner. So the ESOP trustee will have to make a decision about whether the conversion, as proposed, would benefit the ESOP participants or whether its terms need to be modified.

If a decision to switch is made, conversion must occur within 2½ months of the end of the fiscal year. Plan participants are not required to vote on the conversion. This is not one of the required ESOP voting issues because conversion is a matter of individual S corporation owner *elections* rather than an actual vote. A company, however, can choose to have employees direct the trustee as to the voting of the shares.

Note also that the taxable year of an S corporation is the calendar year unless there is a valid business purpose to have a different fiscal year. Avoiding taxes is not a valid business purpose. One allowable exception is that if shareholders owning more than half the shares have a tax year other than the calendar year or are switching to the corporation's tax year. So if a C corporation wants to convert to S, and is more than 50% owned by an ESOP, the ESOP trustee could seek IRS approval for the S corporation to have other than a calendar year tax tear.

Operational Issues for S Corporation ESOPs

Valuation

S corporation ESOPs must pay particular attention to valuation issues. As with all ESOPs, all transactions involving the plan must be at an appraised fair market value. At this point, there is no regulatory guidance about how the special tax benefits the ESOP provides should be allocated in terms of value, but most practitioners agree that the tax benefits should not be counted. That's because those tax benefits are dependent on the company being an ESOP. Appraisals assume a hypothetical third-party buyer. If the buyer purchases the ESOP's shares, there would be no more ESOP tax benefits.

Distributions of Earnings

In most S corporations, distributions are made annually to owners in amounts at least sufficient to enable them to pay their taxes. Even though the ESOP does not have to pay taxes on its share of earnings, it must receive a pro-rata share of any distributions. So if the ESOP owns 30%

of the shares, for instance, and a distribution of $70,000 is made to a 70% owner, the ESOP must get a distribution of $30,000.

In companies where the ESOP is not the sole owner, this can, as discussed above, create cash flow issues. If the ESOP owns most, but not all, of the shares, some companies choose not to make distributions. Instead, owners with a tax obligation have their pay increased sufficiently so that they can pay the tax. As long as their pay does not exceed what the IRS might deem reasonable, this strategy can be effective, even though it means the added amounts paid to the owners will, in effect, be taxed twice (once as income and once to pay the owners' share of earnings). The added tax cost to the company to cover this double tax, however, may be more than offset by the tax savings generated by the ESOP.

Distributions can also be used by the ESOP to repay debt. As noted above, an IRS private letter ruling concluded that only distributions paid on unallocated shares can be used. Distributions on allocated shares would add to the accounts of affected employees. This is different from dividends paid on shares in an ESOP in a C corporation, where dividends on both allocated and unallocated shares can be used.

Where distributions are not used to repay a loan, the distributions will be treated as earnings on shares and will be allocated according to account balances. Some advisors have argued that the distributions could be made according to the plan's schedule for contributions, but there is no ruling that clearly allows this approach. Adding distributions based on account balances may raise issues for the distributional impact of ESOPs on newer employees because most of the benefit would accrue to employees who had larger account balances.

Some companies might want to pass distributions through directly to employees, but this generally is not advisable. These distributions will normally be subject to a 10% excise tax on "early distributions." The pass-through would also require the consent of each employee and would be subject to taxation. Again, some advisors have argued that neither of these restrictions should apply, but there is no specific regulatory support for this as of this writing. It is not clear whether each employee could choose to elect to get a dividend or whether they all would have to choose, but advisors say that the issues created by the pass through would not be worth the potential benefits.

Distributions of Account Balances to Departing Employees

In C corporation ESOPs, employees can demand distributions, and companies choose to make distributions, in the form of company stock. Employees can roll over that stock into an IRA. However, because S corporation rules do not allow for there to be more than 75 shareholders at any one time nor for an IRA to hold stock, S corporation ESOPs must follow specific procedures for making distributions. If an S corporation ESOP wants to distribute shares to employees when they leave (because the company wants to buy back the shares or for some other reason), but wants to give employees the opportunity to roll over the distribution into an IRA, a company can craft its plan so that employees can either get stock and sell it back or get cash and roll it over. If the employee only gets stock that is held very briefly—one day to allow the company to buy it back, for instance—the IRS has ruled that his does not really constitute ownership for the 75-owner test. It also does not create any potential problems with taxes for the employee who rolls the cash into an IRA. The IRS, in a private letter ruling, has confirmed the acceptability of this approach.

Alternatively, the company can just convert the shares into cash before distribution. S ESOP corporation rules specifically allow plan sponsors to eliminate the normal right employees have to demand a distribution in the form of shares.

New Rules for Preventing S ESOP Corporation Abuses

Soon after the law was passed allowing ESOPs to be owners in S corporations and not to have to pay tax on their share of corporate earnings, there was a predictable (if disheartening) rush by some financial advisors to propose ESOPs for clients who really were not interested in sharing ownership broadly with employees. In some cases, this might be for professional firms with one or a few employees. In others, schemes were proposed in which managers would create an S corporation management company to manage a larger operating company. The management company would charge a management fee to the operating company equal to a large percentage of its profits. Because the management company would be structured as an S ESOP corporation, there would be no tax on these profits. In a more complex approach, the management company would include the employees of the operating company in its ESOP (this is allowable in companies that are part of the same control group). Managers in the S corporation would then pay themselves substantial deferred compensation that would escape tax because the S corporation would be 100% owned by the ESOP.

ESOP experts argued that all of these scams were already precluded under general authority granted the IRS to disallow tax shelters that have no valid business purpose other than to shield people from tax. If this test did not work, existing rules in ERISA state "if the plan is so designed as to amount to a subterfuge for the distribution of profits to shareholders, it will not qualify as a plan for the exclusive benefit of employees even though other employees who are not shareholders are also included under the plan."

To provide more specific prohibitions, as well as to buttress the general language giving the IRS power to rule against these scams, Congress included a draconian set of tax penalties in the 2001 tax law.

In addition to the specific rules set forth below, the Congressional conference report directed the IRS to develop regulations to define existing plans as subject to this legislation, regardless of when they were established, if their purpose is "in substance, an avoidance or evasion of the prohibited allocation rule."

The new law is quite complex. The simplest way to describe it is to say that it provides extreme tax penalties for plans designed to funnel most of their benefits to a small group of people who own most of the company, either directly and/or through the plan or through "synthetic" equity (stock options, warrants, etc.). To find out whether a plan is subject to the new law, two steps need to be taken:

1. First, define "disqualified persons." Under the law, a "disqualified person" is an individual who owns 10% or more of the "deemed owned shares" of the corporation or who, together with family members (spouses or other family members, including lineal ancestors or descendants, siblings and their children, or the spouses of any of these other family members) owns 20% or more. "Deemed owned shares" include shares allocated in the ESOP; synthetic eq-

uity such as stock options, stock appreciation rights (SARs), phantom stock, and other equity equivalents; and directly owned shares.

2. Second, determine whether disqualified persons together own at least 50% of all shares in the company. In making this determination, ownership is defined to include:

    a. shares held directly

    b. shares owned through synthetic equity

    c. allocated or unallocated shares owned through the ESOP

    If disqualified persons own at least 50% of the stock of the company, then these individuals may not receive an allocation from the ESOP during that year without a substantial tax penalty. If such an allocation does occur, it is taxed as a distribution to the recipient and a 50% corporate excise tax would apply to the fair market value of the stock allocated. If synthetic equity is owned, a 50% excise tax would also apply to its value as well. In the first year in which this rule applies, there is a 50% tax on the fair market value of shares allocated to disqualified persons even if no additional allocations are made to those individuals that year (in other words, the tax applies simply if disqualified persons own more than 50% of the company in the first year).

For plans in existence before March 14, 2001, the rules become effective for plan years beginning after December 31, 2004. For plans established after March 14, 2001, or for preexisting C corporation ESOPs that switched to S status after this date, the effective date is for plan years ending after March 14, 2001.

Conclusion

The law for S corporation ESOPs provides what is arguably the most favorable tax treatment for any possible corporate structure. This is not an accident or loophole. Congress intended this result because a large majority of its members believe that employee ownership is a valuable way to improve productivity and create a more equitable distribution of ownership. Companies that currently have ESOPs and are principally owned by their plan should almost invariably take a very serious look at converting. S corporations without ESOPs may find setting up a plan desirable as well, especially if their owners do not want to take advantage of the tax-deferred sale to an ESOP available through to owners of C corporations. For those who want to use an S corporation ESOP primarily to benefit a small number of people, while minimizing or bypassing altogether the law's intent to spread ownership broadly, the best advice is not to proceed. The rewards may seem great, but the risks are even greater.

CHAPTER 4

ESOP Feasibility for Closely Held Companies

Ronald J. Gilbert

This chapter examines a number of critical issues that should be addressed in determining the feasibility of an employee stock ownership plan (ESOP). Most, but not all, of these issues are relevant to closely held companies, where the vast majority of ESOP transactions occur. Many of these issues can be determined by the CEO or CFO of a corporation before engaging professional assistance and initiating a formal ESOP feasibility analysis. Eligibility for the ESOP "tax-free" rollover is explained, alternatives to an ESOP are examined, financing strategies are explored, and costs are discussed.

Whenever the subject of ESOP feasibility is discussed, certain basics will always or *should* always be examined:

- Is the valuation acceptable to the selling shareholder(s) and to the ESOP trustee or ESOP committee?

- Will the cash flow of the company support the necessary debt to acquire the block of stock being offered to the ESOP?

- Can the divergent interests of various shareholders be accommodated through the ESOP?

- Will the repurchase obligation costs associated with the buyback of stock from departing ESOP participants in a closely held company be manageable?

- At what level of ESOP ownership are current shareholders comfortable?

- Will the required vote pass-through issues in a private company ESOP, and other corporate governance issues, be acceptable to current controlling shareholders?

- Will the required ESOP contributions fall within the allowed 25% of covered payroll limitation?

In addition to these "standard" items, however, I recommend that a number of other factors be examined in a preliminary assessment to make certain that there are no "red flags" indicating that an ESOP is not feasible or that a better option exists.

Code 1042 "Tax-Free" Rollover Tax Benefit and Eligibility

Tax Benefit

The major benefit for an eligible shareholder selling stock to an ESOP sponsored by a closely held C corporation is the "tax-free" rollover under section 1042 of the Internal Revenue Code (the "Code").[1] However, a significant tax benefit is derived only if there is a substantial difference between the basis in the selling shareholder's stock and the selling price to the ESOP. Most shareholders in closely held companies have a low basis in their stock, and thus most of the selling price of their stock is subject to capital gains taxes. The ability to defer this tax by a sale to the ESOP is thus very attractive. With the current long-term capital gains rate of 20%, and assuming a state capital gains rate of 5%, this tax benefit is worth approximately 25% of the selling price, or $250,000 for every million dollars of the ESOP transaction.

However, to the extent that the stock being sold to the ESOP has a basis that is equal to or greater than the selling price, there is no capital gains tax liability. If the basis is only slightly below the selling price, then the amount of capital gains tax would be minimal. Thus the first item on our "preliminary assessment" or "pre-feasibility" checklist is the basis of stock versus the selling price.

An example of shares that frequently have a basis near the current fair market value of the stock are shares acquired through the distribution from an estate of a deceased shareholder. Thus, children who receive stock from the estate of one or both of their parents typically enjoy little or no tax benefit from selling that stock to an ESOP.

Eligibility for Code 1042 "Tax-Free" Rollover Treatment

Stock with a holding period of less than three years, stock acquired in a certain manner, stock of publicly traded companies, S corporation stock, and certain other types of stock are not eligible for tax-free rollover treatment.

- Stock acquired in connection with employment is generally not eligible for tax-free rollover treatment. An example would be stock purchased by an employee through a corporate-sponsored stock option program. Stock distributed from a retirement plan, such as a 401(k) plan or an ESOP, also is ineligible for tax-free rollover treatment.

- If the corporation is publicly traded, then it is ineligible for tax-free rollover treatment. This includes stock listed on the New York Stock Exchange, AMEX, or NASDAQ. Even being listed on an electronic exchange probably makes the shares ineligible for tax-free rollover treatment. The corporation is also an ineligible shareholder for the tax-free rollover.

- Only voting common stock or convertible preferred that is convertible into voting common stock is eligible to be sold for tax-free rollover treatment.

If, however, a shareholder holds stock that is ineligible for tax-free rollover treatment, it may be possible to have a tax-free recapitalization that converts the existing ineligible stock (nonvoting common, straight preferred, etc.) into eligible stock. The details that determine whether such a recapitalization can be accomplished on a tax-free basis go beyond the scope of this chapter. However, shareholder approval of such recapitalization is normally required. If such a tax-free recapitalization can be accomplished, the holding period of the old security before conversion is "tacked on" and can be used to satisfy the three-year holding period required for tax-free rollover treatment. It is not necessary to start the "holding period" clock over again after a conversion.

If the selling shareholder is eligible for tax-free rollover treatment, elects this treatment, and the sponsoring company consents to the treatment, then certain shareholders are prohibited from receiving ESOP allocations on any stock subject to the tax-free rollover election. This group of stockholders includes selling shareholders, immediate family members, and any 25%-or-greater shareholder. There is a one-year "look back" in determining these percentages. Furthermore, attribution rules apply. For example, the son of a shareholder owning 75% of the company's stock is deemed to own 75% of the company stock by attribution, and thus is ineligible to receive ESOP allocations on stock sold to the ESOP subject to the tax-free rollover election. There is an exception that allows family members to receive ESOP allocations, but the exception does not apply to the attribution rules, so in most cases family members end up being excluded completely from receiving ESOP allocations.

In smaller companies, especially those with a heavy concentration of family member employees, this allocation prohibition may be a serious threat to ESOP feasibility. One reason is that the covered payroll eligible to receive allocations may be reduced to such a low level that it is not possible to make the necessary contributions to repay ESOP debt without substantially exceeding the ESOP contribution limits.

In larger companies, the exclusion of certain shareholders from ESOP allocations is normally not a problem. To the extent that the corporation wishes to make these excluded shareholders whole, it can do so through some type of nonqualified deferred compensation agreement. This agreement can provide the excluded employee with a future benefit equal in value to the benefit that would have been allocated under the ESOP.

Post-Transaction Decrease in Value

Another issue to be addressed with a leveraged ESOP is the so-called "post-deal drop" in value. In many ESOP transactions, the per-share value of the stock will decline after the leveraged ESOP transaction is completed. ESOP appraisers recognize the fact that the corporation now has additional debt, and the requirement to service this debt, which may mean decreased net earnings after the ESOP loan is in place. This post-deal drop in value is recovered as ESOP debt is repaid. Thus, its biggest impact will be the years immediately following the leveraged ESOP transaction.

Alternative Sales Strategies

Even if an individual shareholder owns stock with a low basis relative to the purchase price, and the stock is eligible for tax-free rollover treatment, alternative strategies still may be more attractive from a financial viewpoint.

Sale to a Strategic or Financial Buyer

Any sale to an outside buyer is subject to capital gains tax, unless the selling shareholder does a tax-free stock swap, i.e., the shares owned by the selling shareholder are exchanged for stock in the acquiring company. If the price is attractive and the seller feels that the stock of the acquiring company will appreciate in value, then this becomes another way to sell stock on a "tax-free" basis. If the tax-free stock swap is not attractive, or available, to the selling shareholder, then the strategic buyer would have to pay approximately 33% more than "fair market value" as determined for ESOP purposes if the seller is to net the same amount of proceeds after tax. In some instances, the strategic or financial buyer will be delighted to pay a 33% or greater premium because of the right "fit" of the acquired company. There can be numerous reasons for this premium, but if the only objective of a selling shareholder is to maximize price, then the sale to a strategic buyer should be explored.

Initial Public Offering (IPO)

For some closely held companies, an IPO is another option to be explored. However, even if the company is large enough to consider an IPO (and shareholders are brave enough to try it after recent events in the stock market), and the company's industry and track record make it a candidate, an IPO will usually not provide shareholders with a significant amount of immediate liquidity. This is due to the fact that investors like to see an IPO where most or all of the proceeds remain in the corporation to be used for business expansion, acquisitions, etc. While the sale of a small amount of individually held stock in an IPO is generally acceptable, the larger percentages usually seen in an ESOP transaction (30% to 100%) would usually be unacceptable in an IPO. It is also not unusual for the stock held by principal shareholders in an IPO to be subject to a "lockup" provision. Such a lockup provision would typically prevent shareholders from selling their stock for a specified period of time, such as one or two years, in the public market. Additionally, since the principal's stock has not been registered, its sale after the lockup is usually restricted under Rule 144.

If, however, the major shareholders are willing to liquidate their holdings over a long period of time and feel that an IPO might provide a premium price for the stock of the company, then it should be considered. Individuals who do sell their stock in the public market will be subject to capital gains taxes at the time the transaction occurs.

Financing

Assuming that we have a green light concerning the tax-free rollover and that alternative sales strategies are either unavailable or not in keeping with the objectives of selling shareholders, the next issue for many ESOPs becomes financing. Can the company, in fact, borrow sufficient funds to acquire stock from the selling shareholders? If the financing burden is too heavy for the company to bear, there are a number of strategies to consider.

Self-Financing

To the extent that bank financing is not available to acquire all of the shares offered to the ESOP, one alternative to consider is self-financing. That is, the selling shareholder holds a note from the ESOP, normally subordinate to a loan from a financial institution to the ESOP, that provides the balance of the financing for the purchase price. This approach, however, usually must be complemented with a second loan that the selling shareholder makes against the qualified replacement property (QRP). This is because the selling shareholder, to qualify for the tax-free rollover, must reinvest the proceeds of the ESOP sale in QRP during the period from 3 months before to 12 months after the sale to the

ESOP. Therefore, if all a seller had is a note for some of the stock sold to the ESOP, the seller would typically be unable to acquire the equivalent amount of QRP. Individuals who have other liquid assets, or assets that can be liquidated without adverse tax consequences, would be in a position to acquire QRP without taking a second loan. For most sellers, however, the second loan will be necessary.

Example: the ESOP transaction is for $10 million, representing a 30% stake in the corporation. The bank agrees to loan $8 million. It requires as collateral for the loan the shares in the ESOP, the assets of the corporation not already pledged as collateral, and $4 million of the sellers' QRP. The seller borrows $2 million against the $4 million QRP that is unencumbered and buys an additional $2 million of QRP. "ESOP notes," marketed by some of the major investment banking firms, can be "margined" (borrowed against) up to 90% of their value.

Newly Issued Stock

Another alternative to solving the financing issue is the sale of newly issued stock to the ESOP. The sale of newly issued stock to the ESOP can be in combination with the sale by existing shareholders or can use newly issued shares. The sale of these newly issued shares count in determining the percentage of stock owned by the ESOP, and thus can be used to partially satisfy the 30% requirement needed for the tax-free rollover. At the same time, newly issued shares sold to the ESOP generate working capital for the company. This working capital can be used for expansion, for repaying existing debt, etc. If the company cannot, and its lenders will not, fund the level of debt needed to finance an ESOP transaction and still meet the 30% threshold, this approach can be the solution, and often is. In fact, the largest closely held company ESOP transaction in 1996, for approximately $75 million, employed this approach.

Of course, issuing new shares creates dilution. Thus, the current shareholders and the company's board of directors must get comfortable with the level of dilution that is caused by the issuance of new stock. In some circumstances, the dilutive impact can be reduced by the use of a convertible preferred stock, but this also complicates the capital structure of the company.

Of course, the ultimate test of the dilutive impact of the new share issuance is determined by the return on capital the company ultimately receives. In the words of one of my former finance professors, "If the company uses the capital to build a Mustang, the shareholders will be very pleased that they were diluted, but if the company builds an Edsel, the shareholders will have quite a different attitude!"

Above (or Below) the Contribution Limit

While it is normally understood that other qualified retirement plans, such as a 401(k) plan, must be taken into account when calculating the 25%-of-payroll contribution limit for ESOPs, there are some other assumptions that must be addressed.

Interest Exclusion

Interest is normally excluded from the 25%-of-payroll limit when contributions are made to repay ESOP debt. However, for this exclusion to apply, the company must pass a special discrimination test referred to as the "one-third" test. If the test would otherwise be failed, the eligible payroll of highly compensated employees (HCEs) can be limited in order to pass the test. However, this "limit" solution cannot always fix the problem, because if there is a high level of payroll to highly compensated employees (currently $80,000 and above), capping the payroll of HCEs may reduce the overall payroll to a point where contributions to the adjusted lower payroll will exceed 25% even when interest is excluded. In addition, contributions to repay interest on ESOP debt in an S corporation are not excluded from the 25% limitation.

Contributions Above 25%

More than one potential ESOP has died an unnecessary death, or come close to it, because of a lack of understanding of how contributions significantly in excess of 25% of covered payroll can be made to the ESOP.

As discussed above, interest is excluded from the 25% limit in C corporations if the "one-third" test is passed. To the extent that 25% is still insufficient to service loan principal, dividends are the answer.

Reasonable dividends can be paid on stock held by an ESOP. Dividends paid on stock acquired with the proceeds of an ESOP loan can be used to repay the ESOP debt used to acquire them, are tax deductible for C corporations, and are excluded from the 25% of payroll limitation. Reasonableness is determined by a number of factors, including industry averages and return on investment. However, if the ESOP were to own a convertible preferred stock, the dividend would be determined primarily by the market indicators, i.e., a typical dividend being paid on similar issues of preferred stock. If, for example, the ESOP appraiser determines that for the preferred stock to be valued at par, it needs to pay a 10% dividend, and the value of the preferred stock held by the ESOP is $1 million, then the preferred stock would pay a $100,000 per year preferred dividend that would be excluded from the 25% of payroll limitation. Companies can also avoid the "25% problem" by having the inside loan (the loan from the company to the ESOP) have a longer term than the loan from the bank to the company.

Costs

Costs are sometimes cited as a reason not to implement an ESOP. While costs should certainly be considered and understood before undertaking an ESOP, they are rarely a barrier for profitable companies with 50 or more employees.

The Cost of an ESOP Versus the Cost of Selling to an Outsider

In evaluating ESOP costs, it is also important to look at the cost of alternatives. As in any other service area, there is a range of fees associated with selling a company through a business broker. One of the largest national firms specializing in the sale of privately held companies charges an initial fee of $25,000 to $30,000, which may be refundable, and then a sliding scale of 10% of the first $1 million of sale proceeds, 8% of the second million, 6% of the third million, etc. Other firms may not charge any initial fees, and the percentage of the sale price may be as low as 2% or 3% for multi-million dollar transactions. A bigger consideration may be opportunity costs. There is no guarantee that listing a company for sale will achieve the desired results. What is almost certainly guaranteed is that sooner or later key executives will learn that the company is for sale, and may start shopping their services. Several years ago, one large national firm indicated that it was successful in selling approximately 10% of the firms that are listed. On the other hand, if you can identify a strategic buyer in your industry that is a perfect "fit" for your company, or if you know from prior offers that there's interest in acquiring your company, then there may not be any reason to involve a business broker in the transaction.

If you do receive an offer, it may not necessarily be a lump-sum cash payment. Offers typically involve some sort of down payment, and then ongoing payments, sometimes contingent upon future performance. The buyer may require the continued involvement of selling shareholders for a specified period of time, or on the other hand, may require their immediately departure.

The smaller the company, the more difficult it may be to sell to an outsider. On the other hand, if a company is too small (typically less than 20 or 25 employees) it is probably too small for an ESOP.

Even if the offer is a cash lump-sum payment, what will the seller net after paying capital gains taxes, compared to selling to the ESOP and avoiding capital gains taxes (assuming the seller is eligible for the tax-free rollover)?

Ongoing Costs

Occasionally one sees the "tail wag the dog." That is, companies fear the ongoing costs of operating an ESOP. In fact, operating an ESOP requires the same level of expenditure as operating just about any other qualified retirement plan, including a 401(k) plan, plus an annual independent appraisal. Costs for the independent appraisal can range from $5,000 to $25,000 per year and even more for large or complex situations. However, for most closely held companies, the annual appraisal cost will definitely be in the lower end of the range.

Implementation Costs

This is definitely the area where considerably greater costs are incurred versus other types of retirement plans. Executives today are most familiar with 401(k) plans, where prototype plans are the norm. Because banks and insurance companies aggressively seek to manage the money of employee participants in such plans, they subsidize other services. Unless such a "subsidy" exists through ESOP service firms seeking to provide ongoing recordkeeping services, manage the investment portfolio of selling shareholder, fund repurchase liability with insurance products, etc., then the true costs of implementing an ESOP will be charged by the practitioners involved in the implementation. As a result, ESOP implementation costs in a small company, including an *independent* stock appraisal, pre-feasibility study, legal documents, and employee communications, will probably be $20,000 at a bare minimum, although costs will vary with the experience of the consultants involved and the complexity of the transaction. Larger and more complex ESOP transactions will quickly move into the six-figure area. On the other side of the cost ledger, some companies have employed a "do it yourself" approach to reduce their costs.

Conclusion

Many companies considering ESOP feasibility determine rather quickly that it is a "go or no go." That is, they decide, after speaking to one or two advisors, that either the ESOP will definitely work for them or it definitely will not work. On many occasions over the course of the past 20 years, I have seen these assumptions prove to be erroneous upon close examination. Even companies that have had ESOPs for a period of years and who may be contemplating a second stage transaction will sometimes miss a key point. That "point" can turn out to make all the difference in the world.

A few years ago, my firm met with a company president who had been considering an ESOP for over five years. At the end of a two-hour meeting he produced a list of 40 questions that he had compiled. That is the stuff of a thorough preliminary assessment!

The feasibility of an ESOP is determined by a number of variables, some of which can be very complex. Sometimes, what begins as the "perfect ESOP candidate" never materializes, while the ESOP that "couldn't be done" is. Years ago, the chairman of Kelso & Company (and one of my former bosses), Joseph Schuchert, wrote an article titled "The

Art of the ESOP Leveraged Buyout," discussing certain kinds of leveraged ESOP transactions.[2] There may not be any *art* in an ESOP feasibility study, but its thoroughness, or lack thereof, will certainly determine
the ultimate success or failure of the deal.

Notes

1. See *Selling to an ESOP,* 7th ed. (Oakland, CA: National Center for Employee
    Ownership, 2002).

2. It became a chapter in *Employee Stock Ownership Plans: Business Planning,
    Implementation, Law & Taxation.*

CHAPTER 5

Anticipating and Avoiding ESOP Financing Obstacles

Andrew Sandquist and John J. Cresto

Do prospective ESOP transactions ever fail to close? Absolutely. However, it is not uncommon for any transaction involving financing or ownership transition to stall during negotiations, for a variety of reasons that are not unique to ESOP transactions. The obstacles that arise during the structuring and negotiating of ESOP transactions are generally not insurmountable. Many concerns can be resolved or avoided through proper planning and creative assistance from experienced ESOP professionals. The purpose of this chapter is to highlight common issues that arise during the structuring of an ESOP transaction and to suggest solutions to those issues.

ESOP Lender Issues

A prospective ESOP company's inability to secure financing for a leveraged ESOP is probably the most difficult obstacle to overcome. The inability to secure financing usually results from one or more of the following:

- High leverage or limited debt capacity that restricts a company's flexibility in adopting a leveraged ESOP.
- Lack of mezzanine financing or seller support via a guarantee.
- Inconsistent historical operating cash flows.
- Insufficient cash flows to service debt obligations, or projected cash flows that rely on a "hockey stick" projection to service the ESOP

debt. ("Hockey stick" projections are predictions of future performance that contain unprecedented or unsupported increases in
sales, increases in margins, and so on.)

- Insufficient assets (for example, as may occur with a service company) to secure the ESOP loan obligation, or asset appraisals well
  below the owner's expectations.

An important step that a prospective ESOP company can take to
overcome financial obstacles is to consult with its prospective lender and
its ESOP financial advisors while the transaction is still in the concep-
tual stage. A realistic assessment of the ESOP company's ability to service the proposed ESOP debt is critical. Further, collateral shortfalls can
be anticipated at the outset to determine whether the guarantee of a selling shareholder, the guarantee of company management, the pledge of
sellers' qualified replacement securities, or the reduction in leverage
should be proposed.

Generally, financial institutions will lend an amount of money equal
to a percentage of the value of the company's collateral. This percentage varies from financial institution to financial institution, and also
varies at each financial institution based upon the concentration of a
particular asset category within the borrowing company. Ranges of loan
to collateral ratios are as follows:

- Current receivables (less than 90 days from due date): 70% to 85%
- Improved real estate: 70% to 80%
- Unimproved real estate: 50%
- Inventory: 50%
- Fixed assets: 50%

Prudent preplanning by a prospective ESOP company should include
a realistic assessment of the value of the company's collateral. Appraisals of equipment and real estate should be considered at the preplanning
stages if the prospective ESOP company does not have a good idea of
its current value. Those appraisals likely will be required by the prospective ESOP lender before the closing of financing in any event.

Pledging of a selling shareholder's qualified replacement securities

("1042 securities") can provide a lender with an attractive collateral alternative. The pledge of 1042 securities, however, presents an entirely new set of obstacles, which are discussed at length later in this chapter. Under Section 1042 of the Internal Revenue Code [the "Code"], an owner of a closely held C corporation can indefinitely postpone federal capital gains taxation of the proceeds of a sale to an ESOP that owns 30% or more of the company after the sale if such proceeds are reinvested in "qualified replacement securities," i.e., securities of U.S. operating companies, and certain procedural requirements are met.

Management guarantees to cover collateral shortfalls provide the ESOP lender and the ESOP trustee a level of comfort that may greatly exceed the cash value of those guarantees. Both the ESOP lender and the ESOP trustee recognize that a management team with personal assets pledged to guarantee the ESOP loan maintains a high level of incentive to assure that the ESOP loan is paid off and that the company is successful.

Many of the financing obstacles outlined above can be avoided through creative structuring of the proposed ESOP buyout. For example, a company's ability to secure senior bank financing may be enhanced with a more favorable capital structure that includes either traditional mezzanine financing or equity financing from third party investors. Today, several ESOP-specific mezzanine funds and private equity funds exist across the country to invest in ESOP buyout transactions. Using mezzanine financing and equity financing creates equity dilution obstacles for the ESOP trustee; however, these capital sources can be used to close some of the most complicated transactions.

Finally, a very simple and popular structuring idea used to increase a company's ability to finance an ESOP is to merely decrease the size of the ESOP's purchase during the initial transaction. For example, many ESOP buyouts are structured to occur in stages whereby the ESOP will buy a certain percentage today and retain an option to purchase additional shares at a later point in time. A company's ability to finance an ESOP will always be enhanced if the size of the deal is decreased.

Valuation Issues

Valuation issues are difficult and sensitive matters to negotiate in any transaction and are often more difficult to successfully negotiate in an

ESOP deal. An ESOP is prohibited by the Employee Retirement Income Security Act of 1974 (ERISA) from paying more than the fair market value for company stock, as determined by an independent appraiser. For closely held stock, fair market value is the price at which the stock would change hands between a willing buyer and a willing seller, neither being under any compulsion to buy or sell and both having reasonable knowledge of all relevant facts. While an independent buyer given synergistic benefits associated with merging operations or cutting expenses may be willing to pay more for a given company than an ESOP, ESOPs are prohibited from paying a "premium."

Disagreements may arise between the seller and the buyer over marketability discounts. Many ESOP appraisers argue that the put option for ESOP participants reduces marketability discounts from the common 20% to 40% range for closely held companies to zero to 15%. But other ESOP advisors believe this position is much too aggressive. Moreover, in a fully priced market where purchase multiples approach record levels, a deal may collapse simply because of the ESOP trustee's inability to obtain a fairness opinion on the prospective purchase price, particularly if the multiple exceeds the fair market value threshold.

Extremely aggressive business valuations also can prove to be major obstacles during the negotiation process. Aggressive valuations unsupported by historical cash flows, business factors, or economic factors will undoubtedly cause problems with the ESOP trustee and the ESOP lender during the valuation of company stock for purposes of a leveraged ESOP. Working with an experienced financial advisor in the preliminary planning stages to provide a realistic range of value for the company can minimize these concerns.

Benefit Allocation Issues

Issues with respect to the allocation of benefits under the ESOP should not be insurmountable obstacles so long as experienced ESOP professionals carefully design your plan. It is important to remember that an ESOP is a non-discriminatory plan governed by the Code and ERISA and is subject to the general rules and regulations that control other qualified employee benefit plans (thus, you cannot design an ESOP to benefit only highly compensated employees or certain family members).

There are benefit allocation issues unique to ESOPs that may directly affect a selling shareholder and his or her family. In an ESOP transaction, selling shareholders may elect to defer gain on the sale of their shares by making an election under Section 1042 of the Code. If a Section 1042 election is made, no assets attributable to such stock may be allocated to the shareholder, certain relatives of the shareholder, or any more-than-25% owners, but excluding the shareholder's lineal descendants so long as no more than 5% of the aggregate of all company stock sold by such shareholder is allocated to such lineal descendants. However, the 5% exclusion may not apply to lineal descendants who are considered more-than-25% shareholders by attribution. Thus, the selling shareholder and his or her family have important issues to consider in the design of the ESOP transaction with respect to their ability to participate in the ESOP.

Although benefit allocation issues are not necessarily insurmountable obstacles, they are important factors to consider from the outset for the potential ESOP company. For example, children or other "disqualified persons" may be given additional shares or options to offset their loss of benefits. This can, however, have a feedback effect on value.

Additionally, it is important to note the effect of a leveraged ESOP on the company's equity value immediately following the ESOP transaction. A leveraged ESOP transaction (with a partial purchase rather than a 100% ESOP) will decrease the equity value of the company's equity post-transaction as a result of the ESOP debt utilized to finance the transaction. Accordingly, a drop in equity value will affect other shareholders (i.e., other pre-ESOP shareholders) that may or may not be able to participate in the ESOP. Often, valuation obstacles can be overcome through "make up" or "make whole" provisions whereby such pre-ESOP shareholders will receive options or additional shares to compensate shareholders for the valuation effect caused by the ESOP debt. Finally, any type of "make up" provisions may impact the ESOP appraiser's value of the shares purchased by the ESOP which, in turn, can create other obstacles.

Contribution Limits and Dividend Payments

The repayment terms of an ESOP loan must be considered at the time the ESOP deal is being structured. Typically, a loan is made to the company, which relends to the ESOP. The terms of the two loans need not be identical. The loan is repaid through employer contributions to the ESOP. In addition, dividends paid on shares of company stock acquired with an ESOP loan can be used to make payments on that loan. The maximum amount that a corporation may contribute to an ESOP generally is limited to 25% of the compensation paid to all employees participating in the plan for the taxable year to cover the principal payments on the loan. Moreover, contributions by a C corporation that are used to pay interest on the ESOP loan are fully deductible and do not count toward the 25% contribution limit so long as not more than one-third of the benefits are allocated to highly compensated employees. In S corporations, however, interest does count.

Dividends paid on shares held by an ESOP may be used to repay an ESOP loan that was incurred to purchase the company stock on which the dividends are paid, and such dividends are deductible to a C corporation. The dividends used to repay the loan must be "reasonable," and it may be difficult to meet this reasonability standard if the corporation's cash flow is limited and the post-transaction equity value is reduced substantially because of the transition. (The deduction for dividends on stock held by an ESOP is not available for S corporations.)

Contribution limits can make an ESOP loan impractical in some cases, but appropriate loan structuring, such as having a loan term from the company to the ESOP longer than the term of the loan from the bank to the ESOP, or through the use of dividends, often can solve or alleviate the problem.

Environmental Issues

Virtually every ESOP transaction has some environmental element. Environmental issues are often overlooked in the initial analysis of an ESOP transaction but surface in the diligence process conducted by either the ESOP trustee or the ESOP lender. Because many prospective ESOP companies are not historical borrowers, they may not have conducted Phase I environmental audits on their existing facilities. This is especially true for companies that have not borrowed since the explosion of environmental responsibility legislation in the mid-1980s. Assessing the environmental status of a company's facilities can be time-consuming and frustrating.

Individuals considering an ESOP transaction should assess the potential for environmental issues early on. Certainly, a steel company or chemical plant is more likely to have environmental issues than a service business. However, a steel company or chemical plant is more likely to be thinking of environmental issues on a day-to-day basis. Any company that manufactures or processes goods, and any company that owns real estate, should be aware that a lender and/or ESOP trustee will require a Phase 1 environmental audit of each of the company's facilities before funding an ESOP loan.

Environmental issues rarely are an insurmountable obstacle to an ESOP transaction. Usually a lender can be satisfied if an environmental contamination is quantified, and the borrower has made adequate plans for the remediation of the hazard. It is not unusual for an ESOP trustee purchaser to require some combination of (1) a hold-back from the sale price for the cleanup of environmental contamination or (2) indemnification from the selling shareholders for the cost of clean-up.

Product Liability Issues

Any company that manufactures or distributes products may be subject to product liability claims. The extent of potential claims increases based upon the nature of the goods manufactured or distributed. A manufacturer of table saws is much more likely to have product liability claims than the manufacturer of dishes.

An ESOP trustee purchaser will analyze the potential for product liability claims during the diligence process. On occasion, the product liability insurance carrier for the selling company is weak, or a company's potential claims may greatly exceed the existing insurance. In these circumstances, an ESOP trustee purchaser may require the selling shareholders or the company to purchase add-on insurance to cover any excess claims. The ESOP trustee must be satisfied before the purchase that the company possesses enough product liability insurance or product liability reserves to weather any potential claims.

Change of Control Issues

Selling shareholders often face, for the first time since they founded their companies, the prospect that they will no longer be in control of the day-to-day activities of the business. A selling shareholder who sells a majority interest in his or her company to an ESOP may resist giving up elements of control and yet insist upon a control premium for the stock that he or she sells to the ESOP. This conflict leads to interesting negotiations between the selling shareholder and the purchasing ESOP trustee. Selling shareholders frequently believe that they know best how to run their business. Often they are right. The dilemma of the purchasing ESOP trustee in a majority purchase is to assure that control of the company passes to competent management.

Another conflict occurs when the selling shareholder is required to pledge back 1042 securities to collateralize the ESOP loan. The selling shareholder who has relinquished control of the company to new management can lose his or her pledged 1042 securities to the lender if the company fails. It is natural under that circumstance for the selling shareholder to want to maintain some elements of control of the company, even though he or she has sold a controlling interest to the ESOP. Often, compromises can be reached between the ESOP trustee and the selling shareholder by providing the selling shareholder a seat on the board of directors of the company, providing the selling shareholder a consulting agreement, or in some circumstances paying the selling shareholder a guarantee fee in recognition of the risk the shareholder is taking. On occasion, the selling shareholder will negotiate a right of first refusal with the lender to regain control of the company in the event that the company defaults on the bank loan. This can be accomplished in the form of right of first refusal to repurchase the company's stock from the lender after a default on the ESOP loan. It also can be accomplished by allowing the selling shareholder to cure a default on the ESOP loan and maintain subrogation rights against the company.

Section 1042 Pledge Issues

ESOP lenders, almost universally, have seized upon the idea of obtaining a pledge of a selling shareholder's 1042 securities as a method of making up collateral shortfalls in an ESOP deal. Service businesses that have few tangible assets and no real estate often offer a selling shareholder's 1042 securities as collateral for the ESOP loan. Additionally, the closer a transaction comes to being the purchase of 100% of a company's stock, the more likely that a 1042 pledge will be required to make up a collateral/equity shortfall.

A 1042 pledge presents a number of problems and concerns for the selling shareholder that could turn into insurmountable obstacles if not handled properly. If the ESOP borrower defaults on the underlying ESOP loan and the pledged 1042 securities are taken to satisfy the lender, the seller is put in an uncomfortable position. Not only does he or she lose the 1042 securities to the lender but also the sale of those securities to satisfy the ESOP loan is a taxable event. For example, if the selling shareholder pledges $3 million in 1042 securities against a $3 million loan and the company defaults, the bank may sell the shareholder's securities to satisfy the loan. In addition to losing his or her $3 million to the lender, the shareholder will be subject to a tax on the difference between his or her original basis in the company's stock and the sale price of the 1042 securities. If the selling shareholder's basis in the company's stock is zero, he or she may be subject to nearly $1 million in tax but have no assets to pay that tax. Recognition of this problem by the selling shareholder can lead to a strong reluctance to pledging the 1042 securities to collateralize the ESOP loan.

If the lender insists upon a pledge of 1042 securities to secure a collateral shortfall, the seller can negotiate with the lender and the ESOP trustee purchaser to mitigate the risk. The selling shareholder should seek to obtain from the lender an aggressive release schedule and a release mechanism. As the ESOP loan is paid down, the 1042 securities should be released in kind.

An ESOP lender may require the selling shareholder to maintain a loan-to-value ratio on the pledge of 1042 securities. This ratio is usually between 75% and 80% of the value of the 1042 securities. In the event that the value of the securities decreases over time based upon market fluctuations, the seller is required to maintain the loan-to-value ratio either with a pledge of additional securities or a pay-down of the loan. Some selling shareholders have negotiated a reciprocal provision with the lender so that if the loan-to-value of the pledged securities increases over time based upon market fluctuations to some target amount, the selling shareholder may obtain a release of those securities.

A final issue concerning the pledge of 1042 securities is the circumstance in which the selling shareholder dies while the pledge is in place.

If the selling shareholder does not have other assets to pay estate taxes which are due, the 1042 securities may need to be sold to pay estate taxes. This concern can be eliminated by prudent estate planning on the part of the selling shareholder and may include the addition of life insurance to cover any estate tax shortfall.

Management Continuity Issues

Both an ESOP trustee purchaser and ESOP lender must take a hard look at the post-transaction management of the company. Often, the "management team" of the company before the ESOP transaction was the selling shareholder and no one else. An organization run by an autocratic owner may not be the best candidate for an ESOP, especially if the owner is selling a controlling interest in the company.

The post-transaction management team must be evaluated by both the ESOP trustee and the ESOP lender to assure the continuity of the business and the ability to repay the ESOP debt. If the post-transaction management team is not ready to assume control of the company, the selling shareholder may consider selling less than 50% of the stock of the company while grooming the management for a second-phase transaction.

Trustee Issues

Many companies, in the interest of saving money, appoint an employee as trustee of the company's ESOP rather than hiring an institutional trustee. This situation presents a number of problems that can become insurmountable obstacles. An ESOP trustee owes a fiduciary duty to the plan participants and must put the interest of the plan participants above his or her own. Further, an ESOP trustee is personally liable to each of the plan participants for any breach of this fiduciary duty.

In negotiating the purchase of shares for the ESOP, a company ESOP trustee is put in the uncomfortable position of having to negotiate the best price for the plan participants against the owner of the business. Often the employee ESOP trustee feels loyalty, respect, and an obligation to the owner. Such a trustee finds it difficult to negotiate objectively on behalf of the plan participants and seeks some compromise that benefits the seller to the detriment of the participants.

Some employee trustees have the mistaken belief that simply purchasing the ESOP shares at a price set forth in a valuation report relieves them of all fiduciary liability. In fact, the employee ESOP trustee must make an independent investigation of the company and its prospects for the future as well as of the valuation report and the methods used by the valuation firm in rendering its opinion of the value of the company. Failure to make this independent investigation can subject the employee ESOP trustee to personal liability in the event of a lawsuit by plan participants.

Prudent ESOP lenders look closely at the ESOP trustee in underwriting the loan. Many ESOP lenders require an institutional trustee for transactions that they finance. An institutional trustee traditionally completes extensive due diligence before entering into the transaction and will review the valuation report with a critical eye. This provides the lender with a level of comfort and another set of critical eyes to underwrite the deal. An employee trustee can accomplish the same level of diligence provided that the trustee is represented by independent financial and legal advisors to aid in fulfilling his or her fiduciary duties.

Conclusion

Obstacles can develop in any transaction involving the sale of a company's stock. ESOP transactions present unique and interesting challenges, which can almost always be overcome. Experienced ESOP professionals can assist in providing creative ways to eliminate deal killers in nearly every situation.

CHAPTER 6

Creating an ESOP You Can Live With

Anthony I. Mathews

I do a lot of writing on the intricacies of ESOP design, tax planning, and the legal aspects of plan operation. I seldom put together all the pieces of any stage of ESOP development in a comprehensive overview, though, and the following is my attempt to do so for the preliminary stages of ESOP decision-making and design.

Is an ESOP Right for You?

To begin just a little before the beginning, there are certain issues you would best address before the ESOP has been set in stone (or, for our purposes, the legal documents that formally establish the terms of the plan). If you already have an established ESOP, these may be old news to you. But if you do have an ESOP and they are not old news, a moment of rethinking may be useful. This takes the form of a few pre-commitment questions, described below.

What Type of Plan Is Really Best for Your Company?

There are many ways to approach employee ownership. There is no question that a tax-qualified ESOP brings some amazing tax benefits for companies, tremendous opportunities for employees to share in company ownership, and incredible benefits for selling shareholders. Even given all of that, however, an ESOP is not the only way to get the advantages of employee ownership.

- Gainsharing programs and company value-based bonus programs (like stock appreciation rights and phantom stock plans) can be structured to provide employees with much of the incentive that comes along with ownership (in some cases, more) on a much simpler basis than a tax-qualified plan.

- In addition, there is a wide variety of qualified and non-qualified stock purchase, option, and bonus programs that can be used to provide ownership, usually more selectively than can be provided with an ESOP.

- Simpler qualified retirement plans like profit sharing plans (including perhaps 401(k) plans) or stock bonus plans can be designed to invest significantly in employer stock. These plans can be structured to give the company many of the tax benefits afforded by an ESOP with substantially less regulation and administrative complexity than ESOPs. As a result of changes in the law enacted in 1997, the involuntary investment of employees' 401(k) deferrals is restricted to 10% if the 401(k) plan in question is not an ESOP.

If your primary objective is simply to share ownership or even if your primary objective is employee benefit-driven, these other approaches may well meet your needs with significantly less cost. On the other hand, only an ESOP allows a selling shareholder to defer taxation on gains from sales to the plan by "rolling over" the proceeds into replacement securities, allows companies to borrow money and repay it in pretax dollars, or makes it possible to avoid taxation on the shares of the company an ESOP owns in an S corporation. ESOPs also make investing in employer stock easier from a fiduciary standpoint. But you should consider these employee ownership alternatives, if for no other reason than to assure yourself that they will not deliver the type of program you want. If your choice is an ESOP, then you will go on to consider other issues.

Are You Going to Have to Deal with Any Preexisting Plan Issues?

If you already have a qualified retirement plan in place (some sort of pension or profit sharing plan, for example) you will have to decide how to handle the existing plan. Basically, you can usually choose to convert an existing defined contribution plan to an ESOP or you may simply add the ESOP as a new plan while either freezing or terminating the existing plan or just leaving it alone. The decisions you make here make a real difference in the outcome, both administratively and otherwise.

If your ESOP is being adopted either to replace or coexist with another qualified plan, several pre-adoption issues should be considered. On a purely operational level, if you are amending or terminating existing plans in order to implement an ESOP, you may not have much flexibility in designing the ESOP because of the "predecessor plan" rules (which will require, among other things, that certain prior service be credited for ESOP purposes and that no accrued benefits be decreased in any way as a result of the change), and other requirements to maintain established benefit structures and distribution options (generally called "anti-cutback" rules). Where the ESOP is being adopted to coexist with another plan, it is also important to look at these requirements in the context of ESOP funding commitments. For example, where you have a pension plan with a fixed contribution level that will have to be curtailed to meet ESOP funding objectives, it will take careful planning to design the ESOP in such a way as to avoid terminating the prior plan (perhaps even accidentally).

Almost more important, however, is the fact that existing plans develop employee expectations. Participants view routine administrative features (like the timing of annual statements or benefit distributions) as rights associated with plan participation. In spite of your best intentions, the fact is that virtually every phase of administration will be slower under your ESOP than it was under your prior plan. This is partly due to the valuation requirement, but often, too, the ESOP plays a role in corporate finance that no other plan ever has (or could) and the benefit decisions and communication that had been the exclusive purview of the HR department are suddenly at the mercy of corporate tax planning, which can drag on well into the succeeding plan year. In the meantime, you're stuck.

These are particularly problematic where the prior plan was a profit sharing arrangement. If the money accumulated under that vehicle is being used in the ESOP stock purchase, there are a number of legal and communication issues that will have to be addressed. Whether the prior plan assets are used or not, it is often difficult to convince employees of the value of the ESOP while telling them that their benefit statements and payment of benefit distributions will slow down dramatically.

Where the existing plan is a 401(k) plan, you will have all of these types of problems to deal with and a few more. Where a 401(k) plan has been in place and active for the year, you can easily find yourself in the really uncomfortable position of having to require people either to take back sizable 401(k) refunds or lose out on their rightful ESOP allocation. Neither is easy to sell as an exciting new "employee benefit."

If Preexisting Plans Are Not Being Terminated, How Can You Live with Combinations of Current Plans?

As I said above, many of the difficulties encountered by new ESOP sponsors result from the impact of other benefit plans on the ESOP and vice versa. It is, unfortunately, not at all uncommon to have an ESOP designed and adopted without anyone having examined the interaction of the ESOP with existing plans. Recent changes in the law will correct many of these problems, but nevertheless two especially important issues come up often and need to be addressed.

Limitation Years Section 415 of the Internal Revenue Code (the "Code") limits benefits that may be allocated to individual employees' accounts, based on a 12-month period called a "limitation year." A very important time measurement period for any qualified retirement plan (and don't forget that your ESOP is a retirement plan) is this limitation year. Either your limitation year is defined in your plan document to correspond to a fiscal year or, if it is not specifically defined otherwise, the limitation year will default to the calendar year. The limitation year is important because it is the 12-month period used by each plan to determine the maximum contributions and individual allocations the law allows to be made to the plan, and where the company sponsors more than one plan with different limitation years, the maximum limits are easy to violate. Violating the limits causes a disqualification of the plan, and that is as bad as it sounds.

Basically, the law limits all contributions and allocations to a defined contribution retirement plan to a percentage of salary (25%) or a dollar amount ($40,000 as of 2002, to be indexed for inflation) for a given limitation year. All plans of the employer are aggregated for this purpose, so, when you are calculating the limit for your ESOP with a limitation year ending June 30, for example, you could be forced to include all the contributions made to your 401(k) plan for the year that ended on the prior December 31 as if they had been made to the ESOP. This will almost certainly mean that many employees will not get their full ESOP contribution, and it may also mean that the ESOP cannot be funded sufficiently to meet its obligations. The worst thing about this problem is that really the only way to fix it is not to create it in the first place.

So, unless there is some really compelling reason to do otherwise, just keep all the plan years and (where they are separately defined) the limitation years the same.

Annual Addition and Contribution Limits   Congress was generous in providing tax benefits for leveraged ESOPs, but there are limits. Generally, companies can deduct up to 25% of the total eligible payroll of plan participants to cover the principal portion of the loan and can deduct all of the interest income they pay. Eligible pay is essentially all the pay, including employee deferrals into benefit plans, of people actually in the plan, of $200,000 per participant or less (as of 2002). However, company contributions to other defined contribution plans, such as stock bonus, 401(k), or profit sharing plans, must be counted in this 25% of pay calculation. In addition, "reasonable" dividends paid on shares acquired by the ESOP loan can be used to repay the loan, and these are not included in the 25% of pay calculations. If employees leave the company before they have a fully vested right to their shares, their forfeitures, which are allocated to everyone else, are not counted in the percentage limitations. If the ESOP does not borrow money, the annual contribution limit is now also 25% of covered pay (it had been 15%). Again, contributions to other plans reduce this amount.

There are a number of limitations to these provisions, however. First, no one ESOP participant can receive more than 100% of pay in any year from principal payments on the loan, or more than $40,000 (a number that will be increased for inflation in $1,000 increments), whichever is less. In figuring payroll, pay over $200,000 per year (as of 2002) does not count towards total contribution limits. Second, if there are other qualified benefit plans, these must be taken into account. This means that employee deferrals into 401(k) plans, as well as other employer contributions to 401(k) plans, stock bonus, or profit sharing plans, are added to the ESOP contribution and cannot exceed 100% of pay in any year.

How Are You Going to Fit the ESOP into Your Corporate Culture?

We administrative types may be mostly concerned with the accounting and administrative issues that come up when an ESOP is installed, but the cultural issues can be far larger and harder to deal with. This is really out of the scope of this chapter, but let it suffice to say that you can't just adopt an ESOP and expect everything else to accommodate it. No matter how open your "open door" policy has been, once ownership is involved, everything changes. If you have been running your business largely without input from anyone else and you continue to do so, you can't expect your employees to begin to feel and think like owners just because you tell them to. You have to start treating people like owners before anyone will start feeling like owners.

You may take my word for it that employee ownership, no matter what format it comes in, will change your company. It can make it better or worse, depending on how you handle it, but it will definitely not stay the same.

Have You Made a Commitment to Communicating with Your New Employee-Owners?

Finally, and maybe most important, even though the notion of capital ownership is not one with which employees are automatically familiar, there is no question that "getting the most out of an ESOP" requires a significant commitment to employee communication among employees, management, shareholders and all the consultants who are involved in implementing your plan.

Clear communication during the planning phase can avoid not only problems that result from confusion among the material parties to the ESOP but also the problems that naturally arise when something very unfamiliar is announced very suddenly. We've seen even very generous ESOPs (which were dramatically increasing benefit levels) become major employee morale problems because employees (even relatively high-level management in some cases) were left out of the process until the transaction was finished. And it is important that communications occur at all relevant levels within the company.

In this arena, the most easily (and often) forgotten employees are the middle management/supervisory people who are often the most essential to the success of the plan. It is not at all uncommon, unfortunately, for the highest-level executives and shareholders to get together with consultants and formulate a plan. Then, after the plan has been implemented (without a lot of involvement, if any, from middle management), the chairman of the board heads right for the shop floor to tell everyone they are now owners of the company. Of course, in very short order, the chairman retreats to the executive wing, leaving the shop supervisor and other managers to try to manage a bunch of people who have just been told that they own the place, and who have their own peculiar ideas of what that means.

Anyway, if you are going to be an ESOP company you need to get comfortable with sharing information early on and sharing it in a logical and effective way. This characteristic alone is common to virtually every ESOP success story.

Measuring the ESOP's Financial Feasibility

An ESOP is a complex, highly regulated program affecting virtually every facet of any company that installs one. At the bottom line, though, issues related to the feasibility of an ESOP operationally are largely financial ones. Ultimately, you need the intangible aspects to get the most out of employee ownership, but you need a sound financial foundation to get one going at all. Regardless of how willingly you embrace the notion of employee ownership (or just how much you look forward to the rollover and deferral of all that gain), the bucks have got to be there in several arenas to make it work. Finding out where the bucks stop is a process I call an operational feasibility study. Other practitioners call it other things, but the essence is to help you determine if the ESOP you think you want will actually work in your situation.

Perhaps because they are so complex, many factors are at work in determining the applicability of an ESOP to specific facts. These imply several steps that must be regarded either sequentially or simultaneously as appropriate.

Analyze All the Value-Related Outcomes

Ultimately, no issue has more effect on the installation of an ESOP than the issue of value. Under federal law, an employee stock ownership plan sponsored by a closely held corporation may not enter transactions at prices exceeding "fair market value" as determined by an independent third-party appraisal. This price will frequently be different (sometimes dramatically) from the price a non-fiduciary buyer might be willing to pay for a particular enterprise based on perceptions of motivation of seller, future growth, value added, or other synergies.

Ideally, one of the first elements of the study, then, will be to get at least a preliminary notion of the value you can expect for ESOP purposes. Sometimes, for this purpose value will be assumed based on the seller's sense, an appraisal done for other purposes, the accountant's opinion, and so on. But, it is very probable that the actual appraised value will deviate at least somewhat from any assumed figure. And, if actual appraised value materially differs (in either direction) from your assumptions, the results may be materially affected.

So, at some very early point in the process, you'll need to get an opinion of fair market value from your independent valuation professional.

Now, it is just my opinion, mind you, but I think independent means independent. I don't believe the appraiser (nor the appraiser's parent company or subsidiary or affiliate or brother in law) ought to have any role to play in the process other than appraiser and financial advisor to the ESOP. Conflicts of interest can arise very easily, and any conflict of interest (whether real or just perceived) can invalidate the appraisal, no matter how carefully it might be done.

Determine the Available Corporate Earnings and Cash Flow

The ESOP's ability to service debt (where the ESOP is leveraged) or achieve certain levels of tax benefits (where it is not) ultimately depends on the company's net pretax income and cash flow. Obviously, an ESOP transaction price beyond the servicing ability of corporate cash flow is not feasible, regardless of the value of the enterprise or the structure of the transaction. By the same token, a clear prerequisite for tax benefits is otherwise taxable income. Mindless optimism, however charming it may be, is definitely not a virtue in this circumstance. Overstated earning potential is at the core of most failed leveraged buyouts (LBOs), and one suspects that ESOP LBOs are no exception.

Beyond simple debt service, the study should also take into account any existing or desirable alternative commitments of earnings. Growing a company takes capital, and if your ESOP transaction is going to restrict your company's ability to grow or sustain itself, then maybe the ESOP should be scaled back or rethought.

Compute the Limits Imposed by Covered Payroll

Where the purchaser is an ESOP, a second basic limitation on purchase power and/or debt service ability derives from the covered payroll (i.e., the compensation of employees covered under the ESOP). Based on covered payroll, the law and regulations provide limits on the amount that may be contributed and allocated through the plan.

In very general terms, an employer may contribute to an ESOP and take a deduction for an amount equal to 25% of covered payroll each year on a non-leveraged basis. On a leveraged basis, the company may contribute and deduct up to 25% of covered payroll for purposes of paying principal on ESOP debt and whatever is necessary to fund interest payments if the ESOP is structured such that no more than one-third of the contributions used to service the debt are allocated to "highly compensated employees." Beyond that, no individual employee may have "annual additions" for any given year that are greater than 100% of individual pay (as of 2002), or $40,000 (as of 2002), whichever is less. Annual additions in this case include all employer contributions to the ESOP and any other plan the company might sponsor (except possibly interest contributions as described above); employee contributions to all qualified plans sponsored by the employer (whether 401(k) or whatever); and forfeitures (with the exception of forfeitures of leveraged shares during the years of loan repayment).

Obviously, since these limits are all percentages of payroll, payroll is at the heart of these critical limiting factors. The total compensation of all "employees" of the corporation during a particular year serves as the largest base upon which these limits might conceivably be computed. Compensation will be adjusted for various purposes under law to eliminate deferred compensation, to further restrict "maximum compensation per employee" to $200,000 (as of 2002; this is indexed and adjusted from time to time) as dictated by Code section 401(a)(17), and so on. Covered compensation will also be limited by the terms of the plan. Eligibility criteria will restrict the "covered payroll," as only the compensation of the employees who qualify to participate in the plan may be considered compensation for this purpose. And, finally, where the sellers are taking advantage of the rollover and deferral of gain on the sale and are also employees, covered compensation is further limited due to their and other large shareholders and certain family members being restricted from participation.

In any event, to the extent that a particular transaction might require debt service in excess of these limits, either the debt must be restructured or a mechanism other than contributions must be employed to get sufficient funds through the ESOP. Under current law, dividends can be used to supplement contributions for this purpose. A company in this situation may pay dividends on ESOP shares, which are not subject to these limits and which can be made deductible to the company if they are either passed through to employees directly or used (with some restrictions) by the ESOP to repay an ESOP loan.

Quantify and Account for the ESOP Transaction's Effect on Value and the Other Shareholders

Many ESOP transactions require a level of debt to be assumed by the company (at least as guarantor). That debt can be expected to have an effect (probably negative) on the value of the company. Depending on the particulars, the effect may be substantial or insignificant, but in any case, it will be there. This is an issue in every case, but it can, in certain cases, be a significant enough concern to affect the transaction as a whole. Where less than a total buyout is made, for example, the seller's remaining equity may be dramatically compromised by the transaction. This is particularly an issue, though, where there are multiple shareholders and shares are not purchased uniformly from all shareholders.

Where one shareholder is bought out and others are "left behind," they will have to be aware of the potential for (and willing to absorb) a decrease (hopefully short-term) in the value of their equity. If, in addition, the remaining shareholder is a more-than-25% shareholder and the seller has done a rollover and deferral of gain on the sale, not only is the remaining shareholder's equity compromised but he or she is not allowed to get the ESOP allocations he or she would otherwise be entitled to as an employee. Obviously, there can be pretty serious problems if all of this comes as a surprise.

In any case, it is very difficult to predict the actual effect of debt on value until the appraiser has made a determination given all the facts of the case, so getting that appraiser's opinion on this vital issue early in the process is very important. The post-transaction effect on value and the cost to shareholders of dilution or plan exclusion can and should be quantified before the transaction is set in stone.

Thoroughly Review the Interaction of the ESOP and the Governance Structure of Your Company

How long has it been since you read over your corporate charter or by-laws? Well, if you're going to consider any sizable ESOP transaction, now would be a good time to do so (or, better yet, have your ESOP lawyer do so). The governance structure of your company, including the number of directors, the timing of meetings, any restrictions on authority of officers, voting protocols, or other control-related issues are addressed in those corporate documents. It makes great sense to review them. Especially where an ESOP is about to become a majority shareholder (although the point is the same in any case), these documents will determine the rights and responsibilities of the plan fiduciaries as shareholders and, to a great extent, define the relationships among all the parties after the transaction. Problems here are much easier to correct before the ESOP transaction is finalized.

Figure Out the Effect on Employees and Other Corporate Culture Angles

The question here is "What is the ESOP beast going to do in our living room, and can we live with it?" When you bring an ESOP into your company, many changes occur. (Some of them may even be intentional.) However, it is a pretty good idea to quantify the total effect on employees before the ESOP is in place. Where a qualified plan of some type exists already, it is more than a good idea, it is critical. At this point, you are looking for ways to deal with any issues you have uncovered. Employees' benefit needs, fears, and expectations can all be linked to the installation of this business succession plan—or they can be almost irrevocably turned against the idea.

Although it is always important to avoid predicting the future for employees (you might be guaranteeing it if you do), it is useful to spend the time to determine the effects of the new plan on the existing structures and benefits and communicate the changes before they are finalized. Wherever employees' existing benefits are going to be changed in any way by the installation of the ESOP, it will be perceived as a negative (even if the overall benefit level goes up dramatically) unless you take steps to see that it is not. This sort of thing is not usually taken into account at the feasibility phase of things, but my experience is that this is exactly where this exercise belongs.

I want to reiterate one last point in this area, and that has to do with the forgotten layer of employees in these transactions, the middle managers. As noted above, it is not uncommon for an ESOP to proceed through the design and implementation phase with the involvement of the chairman of the board, the CEO, CFO, etc., on a very confidential basis. Then, immediately after the adoption of the plan, these luminaries go right down into the shop or warehouse floor to congratulate the new "employee owners" and then immediately return to the executive suite to congratulate themselves. This almost always leaves out in the cold a group of people who, for good or ill, have actually been running your company in large part. They are taken by surprise by the announcement; a little insecure about their position in this new, inverted hierarchy; not at all pleased with the prospect of working for the people who worked for them just a few minutes before; and definitely not fans of the ESOP.

If you have an entrenched middle management group, looking it over and planning something to get it on board with the program will be very useful. If these people are enthusiastic about the ESOP, getting the rank-and-file on board will be much easier. If they are not, you have created another giant hurdle to be overcome.

Forecast the Future with the ESOP in Place

It is not too early at this point to also take a look downstream at what the longer-term impact of the program will be. Modeling employees' account balances (even if not for general release) is a good way to give even upper management a sense of what they are getting into. Frequently the bulk of ESOP planning is done with an eye to tax benefits alone. In that case, a series of projections indicating that even your humblest employee will have a six-figure account balance in a relatively short time may have a sobering effect on the process. It may not change a thing you do, but at least it won't be a surprise when your employees start retiring at age 35.

An ancillary concern (although very speculative at this point) is to attempt to quantify the future repurchase obligation before the ESOP is put in place. Where it is possible to do so, evaluating this future obligation will round out the picture of what the ESOP is bringing to the table and at what cost.

All of the above will boil down to a sizable stack of spreadsheets and ledgers and a long-winded narrative on the non-numerical issues. When you have taken a thorough look at the ESOP and everything it will create and effect, though, you will have the information on the table needed to determine whether it works for you.

To summarize, the ideal operational feasibility study should include:

- Conservative (at least realistic) projections of the net income and cash flow of the corporation both with and without the intended transaction.

- Reasonable projections of covered payroll of participating employees.

- Thorough analysis of both pre- and post-transaction value.

- Forecasts of the effect of the intended transaction on employees accumulations and other benefit plans of the employer.

- Forecasts of the effect of the intended transaction on the seller and any other shareholders.

- Analysis of the implication of the ESOP transaction on the governance of the corporation.

- Analysis of the specific communication requirements presented by your employee group.

- A forecast of the accumulation on behalf of employees and, if possible, the future repurchase obligations being created by the installation of the plan.

Some Specifics of ESOP Operational Design

After all the analyzing and forecasting and communicating and planning is done, if the answer is that an ESOP will meet your needs (and you still have the courage to want one), there are still a number of specific design decisions that will have a significant effect on how the plan fits into the company's future. The following is a sampling of the areas in which plan design decisions are made, together with some discussion of alternatives and outcomes.

Determine Who Will Be Eligible to Participate

Under current law, eligibility service may be as little as one hour of service or as much as two years. In all cases, one may also delay entry until age 21. If eligibility service is longer than one year, vesting must be full and immediate upon entry. One year of service for eligibility is fairly typical, with entry occurring either retroactively for an entire plan year or prospectively from the date the criteria are met. Once in the plan, it is typical to require minimum annual hours of service (usually 1,000) and plan year end employment for continued participation.

Where the transaction will allow it, ESOP sponsors might well consider longer eligibility periods (up to two years under current law), even though full and immediate vesting would be required. If the resulting payroll is sufficient to allow the transaction to occur and the effect on the repurchase obligation is not prohibitive, the administration will be much simpler.

Also, final regulations governing plan coverage, discrimination, and other benefit-related requirements published in 1991 have caused some practitioners to rethink conventional wisdom in these areas. Because of the way these requirements interact with the turnover patterns in certain businesses, eligibility and participation criteria that would not have been a problem under law before the regulations may very well result in plan disqualification today. It is very likely, for example, that a plan that requires plan year-end employment and 1,000 hours of employment to qualify for annual allocations could fail the discrimination tests in the regulations if the company experienced even moderate turnover in a given year.

Also, there is no requirement that the eligibility criteria in your plan be linear. For example, there is nothing to automatically prevent an ESOP from having very liberal eligibility criteria in the first years of the plan (e.g., one hour of service in the year in order to get access to the largest possible payroll) and then to have the plan revert to stricter eligibility requirements (e.g., one year of service with prospective entry dates) after the early high funding need is over.

The point is there is nothing automatic about what criteria you use within the legal limitations, and you should consider your options fully and test carefully any choices you make. Also, you should always test every decision in the light of the likelihood that the plan will be around into the future where the company may have very different needs.

Determine the Basis for Allocation of Contributions

Allocation of contributions based on relative compensation is almost always treated as a given in ESOP design, although what is included as compensation varies widely. There's a very good reason for using compensation for this purpose because compensation is the only statutorily approved basis on which qualified plan benefits may discriminate. In fact, no "safe harbors" for ESOP discrimination testing include a factor in allocations for some other criterion (e.g., length of service). Given all of that, though, plan sponsors should be aware that other methods are possible (e.g., points systems or per capita), and one of them might fit better in your circumstances.

In any case, attention to this aspect of plan design is time well spent because, no matter how you design your ESOP to handle allocations, the most significant allocation issues for ESOPs (and therefore the most important design considerations) will relate somehow to compensation.

The problem here comes from the fact that, for different purposes, the word "compensation" can have very different meanings. Frequently, for example, ESOP sponsors will limit or exclude extraordinary compensation (like bonuses or commissions) from compensation for allocation purposes. Or, even more frequently, sponsors will include non-taxable compensation (like 401(k) deferrals) in the allocation base.

There's nothing legally wrong with either of these design features, but in testing for the legal limitations on deductions as well as individual allocations, you must be aware that compensation is determined by the statute and may include or exclude these items regardless of your plan's definition. If your plan is running near the limitations, this can be a problem.

Determine Which Method Will Be Used to Release Shares from the Suspense Account

With a leveraged ESOP, you also have to consider the method for determining how much stock will be allocated each year. ESOP regulations give two alternatives for releasing shares from the suspense account as loan payments are made. The difference between the two methods is that one includes interest in the calculation and the other does not. Many ESOPs use the method that includes interest (known as the "general rule") because it is available to any ESOP, and, if you have an even payment, amortizing loan, it provides even distribution of shares over the period.

With regard to the selection of release method, when you have a rough idea of the terms of your loan, check to see if you will qualify for the special rule. If you can, it makes sense to do hypothetical amortization schedules and test the outcome both ways. Sometimes the results are surprising. Most important, if someone tells you that one method or the other always releases shares more or less rapidly, you are talking to someone who hasn't much experience on the subject. Which method releases shares more rapidly depends entirely on the loan terms and amortization schedule.

Actually, this is not strictly a design issue because your plan document will undoubtedly give latitude to do either. On a particular loan, however, once you have selected the release method, you're generally stuck with it, so it is important to anticipate the outcome before you are committed.

Determine Whether Dividends Will Come into Play and How They Will Be Applied

More than just "typical," with all the fanfare, the deductible dividend has become almost a panacea for any transaction that will not work because of covered payroll considerations. Nowadays, ESOP dividends (whether on allocated or unallocated shares) typically are intended to be used to pay down ESOP debt. For a variety of reasons, often at least some portion of the dividend is passed through to participants directly. ESOP dividends are almost always applied in a way that makes them deductible for the employer. And, leaving aside for the moment that the amount and timing of dividends are controlled by many non-ERISA factors as well, funding an ESOP with deductible dividends creates very tricky administration problems.

In this area, the law is unusually specific. Section 404(k) of the Code provides very specific guidance on how to handle allocations of deductible dividends, although in reality, much of that very specific guidance is unworkable.

In general, dividends are deductible only if they are either paid out directly to employees, used to pay down an ESOP loan (in most cases only the ESOP loan used to purchase the shares on which the dividends are paid), or, starting in 2002, reinvested in company stock at the direction of participants. There are many specific procedural and timing issues related to the deductibility, but our interest here is the unique allocation issues they raise.

To begin with, there is very little if any guidance on the proper basis for allocating shares that were paid for and released from suspense by dividends on shares that were not yet allocated to anyone's account. These released shares could be allocated on the basis of stock account balances, total account balances, compensation, or whatever your plan document dictates. And your plan document must specify how this is to be done. It is fairly easy to determine the effect of different allocation bases for these shares, so if your document does not spell it out already, it is worth spending some time testing the alternatives before you decide.

The rules related to allocating shares released with dividends on allocated shares are much more specific. This process must cause an allocation to a participant's account of shares with a value at least equal to the dollar amount of the dividend that would have been allocated to his or her account if it had not been used to pay down on the loan. This can be very difficult in a leveraged ESOP where released shares have changed in value from their purchase price. You may very well find yourself unable to use these dividends to pay down an ESOP loan if the stock has gone down in value, and to get the deduction, you may have no choice but to pass these through.

The decisions that are made on all these basic design issues related to dividends are significant. The best that can happen if these are left unaddressed is significant delay in administration while everybody tries to figure out what the designers had in mind.

Test Vesting Schedule and Forfeiture Timing Alternatives

The typical ESOP today is equipped with one of two legally required vesting schedules. After 1986, the law required that all qualified plan sponsors adopt a schedule at least as rapid as either "five-year cliff" or "seven-year graduated" vesting schedules. Under five-year cliff vesting, a participant is 0% vested until completing five years of vesting service. At that point, the participant becomes 100% vested, hence the name "cliff" vesting—all or nothing. Under the seven-year schedule, participants must be at least 20% vested after three years of vesting service and must advance at least 20% more for each year of vesting service thereafter, allowing 100% vesting after seven years. The seven-year graduated approach (or some variation incorporating the characteristics of an earlier schedule and meeting the requirements of the law) seems to be the most common, but the distribution of the two schedules seems pretty even.

With regard to the timing of forfeitures, the IRS has indicated that it is improper to forfeit non-vested benefits before the vested benefits have been distributed (or at least a five-year break in service has occurred). A terminee who is 0% vested can have his or her account forfeited immediately, assuming the document so states. Given that, plan sponsors have generally preferred to forfeit non-vested benefits as soon as possible after an employee terminates (even though in many cases that is still quite a delay). Again, though, in this area, the distribution of plans that forfeit as early as possible versus those in which the forfeiture is delayed is pretty even.

My experience has been that for most companies, the two vesting schedules result in essentially the same total vested account balance and repurchase obligation, but they do seem to affect the segment of the population benefiting most. In virtually every case, the five-year cliff causes benefits to accrue more rapidly to higher compensated longer service employees than does the seven-year schedule. In any case, both should be tested before a decision is made because once you have chosen a schedule, you're pretty much stuck with it.

With regard to forfeiture timing, the basic discussion revolves around the problems associated with tracking terminated employees versus the ease of reinstating benefits where a participant terminates and is rehired. Usually, the former has won out in the past, but other wrinkles result here from the new coverage and discrimination tests, which may tip the scale the other way. Under the final regulations related to section 401(a)(4) and 410(b) of the Code, terminees who have worked over 500 hours in a year but whose benefits are forfeited frequently must be included in the gross population for discrimination testing. They may not, however, be included in determining the group of employees benefiting under the plan. Companies with even moderate turnover could find themselves discriminatory when they are required to count these terminees as nonexcludable employees but, because of a rapid forfeiture provision, may not count them as employees benefiting under the plan. This should certainly be considered when determining the timing of forfeitures.

There is also an argument to be made for delaying forfeiture as long as possible from the perspective of planning for the repurchase obligation. A share of stock sitting in the account of a non-vested terminee is not a liability (unless, of course, you rehire the person involved). Delaying the forfeiture reallocation for the full five breaks in service creates a large pool of stock in this category and can have a significant impact on your overall repurchase obligation. On the other hand, if the ESOP is terminated, you may wind up having to fully vest all these ex-employees and distribute benefits to them that would otherwise have gone to current employees.

Determine Distribution and Repurchase Policies for the Long Term

According to recent studies by the NCEO (and consistent with my experience), typically the ESOP is used by the company to repurchase distributed shares, and in general distributions are delayed for some time after termination (often as long as possible under the law) to slow down repurchase cash flow. While these positions seem to make sense to a large number of ESOP sponsors, there are serious issues to consider regarding both these policy decisions.

Often, when you take into account that unless you sell the company or have an IPO, any share the ESOP buys will have to be bought again later, the pretax advantage of using the ESOP to repurchase shares diminishes. In many cases, the company (and the remaining ESOP participants as well) may be much better off retiring distributed shares even if they are later recontributed to the plan.

By the same token, delay of distributions may or may not give the best outcome. If your stock is appreciating, the longer you wait the more it costs to buy the shares back. If the appreciation occurs at a rate that exceeds earnings on other investments, you may well fall behind in your funding strategy.

In any case, these policies should be investigated and formalized as soon as they reasonably can be so that you avoid getting stuck with unlivable results.

Finally, if you examine all these things closely and thoughtfully, many of the design mistakes that plague some ESOP companies can be avoided.

Conclusion

If you are in the very beginning of establishing an ESOP, the next few months will likely be almost overwhelming. There is tremendous expense in time, money, and emotional energy involved in getting through the maze of requirements, but at the other end, if you take the time and get the help to do it right, you will be pleased with the result of employee ownership. ESOP companies can be very exciting and profitable places to work.

CHAPTER 7

ESOP Valuation Issues

Corey Rosen

The law requires that all ESOP transactions involving the stock of the sponsoring employer be based on a current appraisal by an independent, outside valuation expert unless the company's stock is readily tradable on an established securities market. Because most ESOPs are in closely held companies where such independent appraisals are required, valuation is an important issue in the ESOP world. (Public companies with a ready market for their shares do not need a valuation for ESOP purposes; they simply use the market price.)

Who Performs the Valuation

An independent, outside professional must perform the valuation. There are no standards to determine what constitutes a professional, other than, as the proposed regulations on valuation put it, someone who customarily does appraisal work. Appraisers do get certified by various appraisal organizations, but these certifications usually only involve short programs or examinations, not professional degrees or tests of detailed competence. However, appraisers who are chartered financial analysts go through a much more extensive program requiring passing very demanding exams. "Independence" has also not been defined, but most consultants argue it means hiring someone with no other business relationship with the company, including the firm's CPA or an appraiser who works with a lawyer to set up the ESOP. Aside from these legal requirements, an appraiser should be sought based on specific ESOP experience.

Some lawyers say that the company should not discuss valuation approaches with an appraiser beforehand because it indicates "appraisal shopping," but most believe the trustee must have a clear idea of what assumptions the appraiser will make in terms of such factors as control premiums, discounts for lack of marketability, the definition of the interest to be valued (a minority, non-marketable interest, for instance), and the repurchase obligation.

The Basic Elements of an Appraisal

An appraiser will look at several factors. These include projected future cash flows and profits, book value, market conditions, debt, management, technology, etc. Data on comparable public companies will be collected, particularly financial ratios such as price/earnings ratios, assets/earnings, ratios, etc. These ratios help determine how much the company being appraised is worth (if comparable public firms have an average 7:1 P/E ratio, for instance, the appraised company could be valued at a similar ratio, adjusting for the typical higher price-to-earnings ratios found in public companies), but most appraisers also factor in net asset value and/or discounted future cash flow or earnings (that is, how much is the right to future revenue streams is worth in terms of a lump sum today). These factors will be blended to come up with a number. Obviously, different appraisers will come up with different values.

From there, the appraiser will adjust the value to reflect discounts for lack of marketability if the company is private (it is harder to sell shares in a private firm than a public firm), lack of control (people pay a premium for control rights), and, for some appraisers, the repurchase obligation. How much, if any, discount is taken varies with the appraiser. For this reason, it is important to discuss these assumptions beforehand. These discounts are discussed in more detail below.

Information the Appraiser Will Need

There are no legal requirements for what must be included in an ESOP valuation. For the valuation to have merit, however, most appraisers will want three to ten years of financial statements, preferably audited or at least reviewed; three to five years of projected financial statements; interim statements as close to the valuation as possible; a list of all lines of business, assets, off-balance sheet assets and liabilities; lists of main customers, suppliers, and competitors, legal agreements affecting the company and its owners (such as by-laws and buy-sell agreements); a list of assets, capital and depreciation expenditure records; major contracts; compensation schedules; a history of any stock sales and offers; and any other information that could affect how much the company is worth.

In addition, the appraiser will want to visit the company and talk to key people. In very complex cases, interviews with customers, suppliers, and industry experts could be in order, but most valuations will not take this step.

Failing to provide adequate information, or providing misleading information in a way that could affect value, is a serious offense that could lead to lawsuits by the participants or the government, as well as the loss of tax benefits and the imposition of penalties. ESOP fiduciaries are generally responsible to make sure the valuation consultants receive the proper information.

Factors That Can Reduce Per-Share Value
Control Premiums and Lack of Control Discounts

A control premium is simply the mirror image of a lack of control discount. A shareholder owning less than controlling interest in a company has an investment worth less than a shareholder owning a controlling interest. Controlling shareholders can use the assets much more freely, selling them to other buyers, taking larger or smaller dividends, selecting the strategic direction of the company, etc. In takeover battles in public firms, the run-up in price when an offer is made is usually simply a function of someone offering to pay a premium for control.

Owning a majority of the stock is one level of control, but some issues in companies require more than a majority vote, so shareholders owning enough to block a transaction, but not enough to exercise day-to-day control, may pay a premium for this lower level of control, although not as high a premium as they would pay for majority control. Similarly, an additional premium would be paid for owning enough stock to control all issues.

Just owning shares is not enough, however. Valuation guidelines for ESOPs say that for the ESOP to pay a control premium, the trust must have "control in fact." While this has never been defined in any useful way, it would clearly exclude a situation where the ESOP trustee was controlled by another shareholder. The trustee in that case only has nominal control and should not pay a premium for it.

As to how much the control premium is worth, there is no simple answer. Control premiums are often in the range of 25% to 35%, but can be higher or lower depending on the level of control involved and how valuable that control is given the assets involved. For instance, a company whose assets are encumbered by long-term covenants (such as with lenders, courts, or regulatory agencies) would have a lower control premium than a company whose assets are not. There is also a lot of variation from one appraisal firm to another.

There is no consensus on whether the ESOP can pay a control premium if it owns a minority position but plans to acquire a control position later. Many valuation consultants say an ESOP can pay a control premium if it has a specific option to buy control in a reasonable time, usually three to five years or less, and obtains an irrevocable proxy to vote a sufficient number of additional shares to take over voting control. Others argue this should not be the case; that the ESOP should only pay for control when it acquires it. There is no right or wrong approach, but the valuation process should, in any event, use the same assumptions year after year about control.

If the ESOP already has control, it usually may pay a control price for additional shares if there is an agreement that it will, and if the value is used consistently for all ESOP transactions, including repurchases of shares from employees. Again, however, different appraisers have different philosophies.

Lack of Marketability Discounts

Owners of shares in closely held firms cannot sell their shares as easily as owners of publicly traded ones. Because of that, their shares are worth less. Marketability discounts vary considerably, but they typically range from 10% to 30% in ESOP transactions. Again, the variation is explained by the particular facts (Are their other potential buyers? Is the ESOP a reliable buyer able to make the payments needed to make the purchase?) and differing appraisal philosophies.

Some appraisers argue that the put option in an ESOP reduces or eliminates the marketability discount; others argue it depends on the plan's proven ability to repurchase shares; still others say it depends on whether the contributions to the ESOP needed to repurchase shares increase or decrease what the company would otherwise spend on benefit plans; while some appraisers contend that the put option is not the same thing as a liquid market and should provide only a small reduction in the marketability discount. Passionate arguments are made on all sides.

The NCEO has taken a position on this, namely that the put option itself does not create a market unless the company shows it has (or can contribute to the ESOP) the funds to satisfy the put. If that is the case, however, the commitment of these funds to a non-productive purpose should reduce the company's value unless they constitute no more than what would be contributed to employee benefits plans anyway if the ESOP were not in place. Even then, some marketability discount should remain, because the put option is a restricted right to sell shares, subject to all the rules, delays, and limits of the ESOP distribution formula. Not to take this approach, we believe, means the company will overpay for the stock, impeding growth and harming the interests of future employee owners.

Many people disagree with this, however, arguing, for instance, that the company could always sell or, in some cases, go public to provide liquidity, or that not to pay the highest price possible is unfair to current participants.

Almost everyone agrees that there is a tendency in valuations to make favorable assumptions up front (such as assuming the put eliminates the marketability discount) to provide sellers a high price. Trustees need to be very wary of this, however, because it can harm the interests of plan participants down the road.

Liquidity Discounts

This is similar to a marketability discount and is often not taken in closely held firms. It refers to the cost of becoming "liquid" for investors, typically by going public or selling. These transactions involve legal and transactional charges that can add up to 3% to 7% or more of the value of the transaction. Liquidity discounts are not commonly found in valuations where it is assumed that the company will resolve its marketability issues by selling or going public, so the presence of a liquidity discount would often be accompanied by a reduction in the marketability discount.

The Effect of ESOP Debt on Company Value

The debt the ESOP takes on is accounted for as debt of the company. Because the company now has this debt showing up on its balance sheet, its value is reduced. It is generally not reduced, however, by the face value of the debt. For one thing, the ESOP borrowing brings certain tax advantages to the company that should be capitalized and reduce the impact of the debt. Second, the debt is one that is repaid over several years. If the company's earnings exceed the cost of the debt, then the impact of the debt should be discounted to reflect that.

Frequency and Timing of Appraisals

The law requires at least an annual appraisal. The only exception to this is that if there is no stock contribution or benefit distribution in a given year, a full-blown valuation is probably not needed, but the trustee must make a determination that the existing valuation is appropriate. If something significant has changed, then a determination must be made about whether a new appraisal is needed.

Technically, any ESOP transaction or allocation should be at the current appraised value, meaning companies should try to time their ESOP activity with the appraiser's report (buying shares when the report is issued and the trustee determines it represents the fair market value). In practice, this may be impractical in some cases. There are a few ways to deal with this. If the issue is allocating stock, the allocation can be backdated to the determination of value. For instance, imagine the plan year ends in December, as does the fiscal year, and that the valuation is completed March 15. The company can make the allocation in March but credit participant accounts as if the allocation had been made in December at the value that applied to December 31.

If the issue involves a purchase, and the valuation is more than a few weeks old (there is no precise time period), then the trustee should at least certify that there are no material changes in the company or its markets that would cause the ESOP to pay more for the stock than it is currently worth. If the valuation is too conservative, and the ESOP pays less, that is not normally a problem, at least as far as ERISA is concerned. This trustee opinion may require a brief analysis by the appraiser. If conditions have changed materially, however, a new appraisal will be needed.

If shares are distributed under an ESOP a few months after the most recent appraisal, a thorough appraisal (what would be done at least annually in ESOP companies) is not needed, but the trustee must determine whether the old appraisal is valid or can be updated without an appraisal. The trustee must be able to show this is a valid price. Because the fiduciary still is responsible for making sure the price is fair market value, however, not getting an appraisal from an independent appraiser is risky. For instance, how can the trustee decide if a valuation is needed without professional advice? What number would be put on the company's 5500 form?

The Effect of Other Equity Investors on an ESOP Valuation

So-called "multi-investor" ESOP transactions raise the difficult issue of "equity allocation." There is no ESOP valuation subject so controversial. The problem can be illustrated by an example. Imagine that a group of employees wants to buy their company. A lender is willing to loan them up to 70% of the asset value of the firm, provided they agree to wage and benefit concessions. This will provide 60% of the asking price. The lender also requires that management put up some of its own money because its wants them "on the line." That will provide another 10% of the price. The remaining 30% will be obtained from an equity partner, perhaps another company or private investors who are willing to put up cash.

The valuation problem is to assess how much each investor should get. The simple view would be "dollar for dollar." The ESOP is putting up 60%, so it should get 60%, while the managers get 10%, and the investors get 30%. The cash investors will argue, however, that they are putting their assets at risk; the ESOP will repay its debt out of future earnings, and the participants in the plan will not be liable if there are losses. The employees argue that they are taking concessions, and that the ESOP provides important tax benefits as well.

In the 1980s, some leveraged ESOPs were put together in which equity investors got a different class of stock that provided them with much more ownership for fewer dollars, relative to the ESOP purchase. The Department of Labor took legal action to challenge some of these, arguing for the "dollar for dollar" approach. That position made multi-investor ESOPs virtually impossible to put together; investors wanted more for an investment with those kinds of risks. Over time, some approaches to this problem have been developed that use convertible preferred stock for the ESOP, allowing it to pay a higher price for its interest in the company than other investors, or providing investors with stock warrants (the right to buy additional shares at a fixed price in return for buying some shares at market price), or stock options. Many ESOP advisors, however, are reluctant to create multi-investor approaches for fear that they will be challenged.

The particular valuation techniques used to allocate equity involve assessing comparable rates of return for investments of similar risk, capitalizing the value of future ESOP tax benefits and/or employee concessions, and complex mathematical models to assess the present value of income streams to various investors.

Valuations vs. Fairness Opinions

A valuation assesses either the fair market value of an enterprise or of the ESOP share of the enterprise, depending on its purpose. A fairness opinion determines the fairness of a transaction to participants in the transaction. In simple transactions, this is not an issue. Where there are multiple owners, and especially where there are different classes of stock or different groups are putting up different kinds of investments (one group cash, one group borrowing money, an ESOP borrowing money the company repays, employees putting up wage or benefit concessions, etc.), fairness is more complicated. If one investor puts in $1,000,000 in cash and the ESOP puts in $1,000,000 with borrowed money to be repaid out of future earnings, what is a fair price for both to pay? These and similar situations call for a professional financial advisor to opine on the fairness of the transaction, but the ESOP trustee must ultimately make the decision. Fairness opinions are not legally required in ESOP or other transactions, but are highly advisable in complex ones.

With a fairness opinion, a financial advisor is retained to advise the ESOP fiduciary to determine if the offer to buy stock is fair to all parties. The advisor will assess present and future prospects for the company, the existence of other alternatives to the sale, the ability to obtain financing for the transaction, and the overall effect of the proposal on the company's various constituencies. The report may just be a letter with an opinion, outlining the methods used to arrive at the judgment.

Cost and Contracts

It is important to note that the appraiser is hired by and reports to the trustee, not the company. The appraisal is done to protect the ESOP, not maximize the sale price for the owner(s). Nonetheless, it is the company that will pay the fee. Initial appraisals will typically run $8,000 to $15,000 in conventional transactions; more complex transactions (such as with multiple investors or multiple lines of business) will cost more. Repeat appraisals will be less costly, typically two-thirds to half the initial cost.

CHAPTER 8

Choosing Consultants and Trustees

Corey Rosen

One of the questions we at the NCEO are asked most often is "How do I choose consultants to set up my ESOP?" There is no shortage of people claiming to have expertise in this field. All too often, we hear from companies whose advisors told them of their profound understanding of the law, only to find later they were not as expert as they claimed. Choosing well-qualified, experienced people is essential; the penalties for plan disqualification, improper valuations, inadequate repurchase liability analyses, and other problems can be severe for owners and employees. While there are no formulas for choosing your advisers, there are some key questions to ask.

In picking a consulting team, you will need, at least, a valuation specialist, an attorney to draw up your plan and possibly negotiate with a lender, and a plan administrator. You may also want an independent trustee, an investment banker or financial advisor, and a communications-participation consultant as well. Some people find the best approach is to hire a "packager," someone who can bring together a team of consultants to do each of these tasks. The packager would serve as your primary contact, making life simpler, if more costly. If you go this route, make sure that all of the people the packager is bringing in are experienced and competent.

There also are "turnkey" firms that provide all of the required services except, perhaps, valuation. For this, they usually refer the client to an appraiser with whom they work. We recommend, however, using a completely independent appraiser. The law requires an independent appraisal, and while this has never been specifically defined, we believe an appraiser working as part of a group has too much of a potential bias to provide a price that can help the deal go through. The conflict of interest is even worse, of course, if the appraiser works for the turnkey firm itself. Also, if you hire a turnkey firm, you should make sure that each of the advisors is independently experienced and competent. Ask yourself whether you would hire each of them to be on your ESOP team if they were at different firms. If the answer is "No," then you should not employ that firm.

Choosing a Valuation Consultant

For privately held companies, often the first step in deciding on an employee ownership plan is getting a valuation. If the value of the stock is too low to be acceptable, or too high to be affordable, there may be no reason to proceed further.

ESOP valuation specialists charge widely varying amounts. Part of the difference is the firm's reputation. If your valuation is ever challenged, that reputation may be worth paying for, even if the work performed is the same as another firm with a lesser reputation. Another part of the fee difference is how many people at the firm review the appraisal. More reviews may mean more accuracy.

Appraisers also vary in terms of their philosophy towards ESOPs. Different appraisers will place different discounts or premiums on majority or minority stakes, on the presence of a put option (this could increase the marketability and hence the value of shares), on the repurchase obligation (this will reduce share value), and other ESOP-specific factors. Appraisers also vary in the emphasis they place on different valuation methods, such as discounted earnings or comparable companies. You need to tell prospective appraisers what you want to do with your plan, then find out what basic assumptions your appraiser will bring to this potential transaction. There is not a single right or wrong way to arrive at a value, but the different approaches can result in values more or less appropriate to your needs and opportunities.

Finally, you should request a statement from your appraiser indicating if the firm has ever been challenged on an appraisal and what the results were. The challenge may have been unfair to the company, of course, but you should know about it. You should also know how many ESOPs the firm has valued.

Choosing a Lawyer

Picking an attorney is somewhat simpler. Like valuation people, however, they differ in philosophy. While this will not have as dramatic an effect as with an appraiser, your attorney should share your approach to ESOPs. For instance, if your attorney believes it is essential to have an independent trustee, only limited employee voting rights, and union employees should be kept out of the plan, but you think the opposite, you will have to spend a lot of time discussing this. At $150 to $300 per hour or more, you could spend your money more productively.

Second, make sure your attorney is providing you with a fee and time schedule that is realistic and comprehensive. An attorney may quote a fee that only represents initial plan design, not all the filings, filing updates, and question answering that will need to be done after the plan is written. Schedules for completion may be hard to predict, but avoid people whose time frame seems unusually optimistic—delays are almost inevitable.

Finally, ask for references from prior clients. If there aren't any, find another attorney. If there are, call a few and find out whether the work was competent, timely, and within estimated charges.

Choosing a Plan Administrator

Much of plan administration is record-keeping, so experience and price can be the key determinants here. Part of your administrator's burden, however, should be to perform and update repurchase obligation studies. Good administrators should have their own data banks of ESOP clients on which to base these studies. Studies that rely on too many assumptions or theories, rather than what actually happens, may be misleading. If you have a 401(k) or other retirement plan, you should hire an administrator who can handle both. This will help prevent inadvertent violations of plan testing rules.

Other Consultants

You may also need separate people to help with investment banking, feasibility studies, communications, or employee participation issues.

Investment banking is very expensive, generally charged at a percentage of the financing secured, and is rarely necessary in the typical smaller ESOP. More complex transactions, such as where there is a need to bring in equity investors or mezzanine debt, often do require investment-banking services. The need for other advisors depends on what you can do in-house. If you do decide to hire these people, philosophy is, again, as important as price and experience.

Choosing a Trustee

Selecting a trustee for an ESOP is one of the most important decisions made before a plan is established. Trustees vote and tender ESOP shares (although they may be directed in this by management or employees), oversee the valuation of the stock, are responsible for investment of non-employer securities in the ESOP, pass judgment on the soundness of ESOP purchases, and generally are responsible for the operation of the plan in the best interests of employees.

There are no legal requirements for who selects the trustee. In most cases, management or the board selects the trustee, but, occasionally, an employee committee will make the choice; more rarely, outside advisors, investors, or creditors may either choose or approve a trustee.

Anyone can serve as a trustee. Typically, the trustee is either an outside institution with trust experience, most commonly a bank or trust company; an officer of the company; or a trust committee, usually made up of company officers and/or employee representatives.

A directed or "custodial" trustee does not act as a fiduciary but rather operates the plan as instructed by the fiduciaries (for example, a bank may serve as a custodial trustee that receives instructions from a trust committee at the company). This service comes at a high price but does not relieve the fiduciaries of responsibility, so we do not recommend it.

Assuming the trustee does act as the fiduciary, having an independent, outside trustee provides some protection should the plan's operations be challenged. Presumably, such a trustee in this circumstance will make an independent decision without the conflict of interest an insider would face. On the other hand, an outside trustee can be very costly (anywhere from several thousand dollars to hundreds of thousands of dollars a year, depending on the size of the transaction and the ESOP's assets), and the very independence of the trustee could diminish insider control in critical circumstances.

A reasonable compromise for many companies is to have an inside trustee or trust committee for normal operations, but appoint an outside trustee for special circumstances that present strong conflicts of interest, such as an acquisition proposal.

Clearly, the trustee should not be someone without a good working knowledge of the law and the plan. Also, someone who is selling stock to the plan should never act as the sole trustee. The trustee should be negotiating for the best deal for participants, and such a person has an obvious conflict of interest that would be difficult to justify in court.

Where to Start Looking

NCEO members receive access to the referral service in our Web site's members-only area, a searchable database of hundreds of fellow members who are service providers in employee stock plans and ownership culture. Certainly, this is a good place to start. The NCEO does not endorse anyone listed, but we do know most of the consultants involved in this field. Using our referral service is preferable to relying on local people who claim expertise; we have heard too many horror stories from people who used this approach. While having people nearby is convenient, location should be a lower priority than other factors. Much of the work can be done on the phone, through the mail, or by fax.

Workshops and conferences are another good place to meet consultants. There are now over 100 ESOP meetings annually sponsored by various groups, including an annual conference and introductory workshops the NCEO holds nationwide. They, as well as various publications, are also a good way to become educated before starting your plan. The best way to keep consultant costs down is to personally understand how your plan will work.

Finally, if you are an NCEO member, we can put you in touch with ESOP companies in your area. Their recommendations are usually valuable.

CHAPTER 9

ESOP Distribution and Diversification Rules

Scott Rodrick

Distributing ESOP benefits is a central responsibility and function of the plan, and it raises many issues. There are a number of interlocking rules that apply to various facets of distributions. This chapter covers the main rules. It also covers diversification, which offers ESOP participants nearing retirement the opportunity to diversify their ESOP investment by moving part of their account balance out of company stock; one way this can be accomplished is by distributing the amount to be diversified.

Companies have a certain amount of flexibility in how they may structure their distribution policies, and may be more generous than the law demands them to be (for example, not delaying distributions as long as is legally permissible). However, it is important to remember that the ESOP plan document (which must adhere to the rules, such as those set forth here) controls, and that if the plan document does not authorize a particular thing the company wants to do with respect to distribution, then the company cannot do it. Therefore, the company and its ESOP attorney (and possibly other consultants) should discuss these matters and make the appropriate plan design decisions before the ESOP attorney drafts the plan and the company establishes its ESOP. A company may modify at least some of the distribution options in a nondiscriminatory manner (e.g., it cannot treat similarly situated participants in a different manner), but it is not always clear what is permissible.

The author thanks Karen Ng of the San Francisco, CA, law firm of Trucker Huss for her assistance in preparing this chapter.

The Special ESOP Rules

ESOP benefits are mainly paid to participants after their employment with the company terminates, whether because of retirement or other reasons. There are two sets of rules that govern the main ESOP distribution issues: the special ESOP rules and the general rules that apply to all qualified plans such as ESOPs. Section 409(o) of the Internal Revenue Code (the "Code"), enacted in 1986, sets forth the special ESOP rules, which apply to distributions attributable to stock acquired by the ESOP after 1986.

Retirement, Death, or Disability vs. Other Terminations

As far as how soon benefits are paid, the special ESOP rules distinguish between *retiring* (or death or disability) on the one hand, and simply *leaving* the company due to other reasons (such as quitting or being fired) on the other hand. When a participant retires, becomes disabled, or dies, the ESOP must begin to distribute vested benefits during the plan year following the event (unless the ESOP plan document permits the participant to elect to defer receipt of the distribution). When employment terminates for other reasons, however, the beginning of distribution may be, and often is, delayed for some time. It must start no later than the sixth plan year after the plan year in which termination occurred (unless the participant is re-employed by the same company before then or the ESOP plan document permits the participant to elect to defer receipt of the distribution).

Lump-Sum vs. Installments

Under the special ESOP rules, distributions may be made in a lump sum or in substantially equal installments (not less frequently than annually) over a period no longer than five years. This actually means six annual payments, not five: for example, a distribution beginning in 2002 and ending in 2007 (i.e., five years later) will have payments in 2002, 2003, 2004, 2005, 2006, and 2007. However, this five-year period may be extended an additional year (up to a maximum of five additional years) for each $160,000 or fraction thereof by which a participant's benefit exceeds $800,000 (as of 2002; these figures are indexed by the IRS for cost of living adjustments).

What this means is that an employee may have to wait a long time to receive benefits. Take someone who becomes 100% vested in his or her ESOP benefit and then quits: he or she may have to wait five years until distributions begin (assuming this period is not further delayed by waiting for an ESOP loan to be repaid, as described below) and then another five years to receive distribution of his or her entire ESOP benefit. However, most participants do not have to wait that long. A 1999 survey conducted by the NCEO found that 77.1% of all ESOPs paid out in full within one year of retirement rather than using installments. When employment was terminated for reasons other than retirement, 32% of the companies distributed within one year, 40.2% distributed after a five-year delay, and 27.5% distributed after a delay of between one and five years.

Delaying Distributions of Leveraged Shares

Notwithstanding the above rules, the special ESOP rules provide that a leveraged ESOP (at least in a C corporation) may delay the commencement of distributions of shares acquired through the loan until the plan year after the plan year in which the ESOP loan is fully repaid. However, the general qualified plan rules may mandate an earlier distribution (see below).

If the company makes distributions in installments, and those installments have been delayed by waiting for the ESOP loan to be repaid, all the installments must be completed by the later of the end of the plan year after the plan year in which the loan is repaid, or the date they would be completed if there had been no delay. For example, take a participant who quits in 2002 at age 35. Ordinarily, the ESOP could wait until 2008 (the sixth year after termination) to begin distribution, and then make distributions in installments over a five-year period from 2008 to 2013. However, the participant's vested ESOP benefit consists of shares bought with a loan that is not repaid until 2010. The ESOP can wait until 2010 to commence distributions to this participant, but the ESOP cannot make distributions over a five-year period and delay the final installment until 2015; instead, it must complete them by 2013.

General Qualified Plan Rules

ESOPs are subject not only to the above ESOP-specific rules but also to rules that affect all qualified plans.

Basic Rule

Under Code Section 401(a)(14), unless the participant chooses otherwise, the plan must begin distributing benefits no later than the 60th day after the end of the plan year in which the *latest* of the following events occur: (1) a participant reaches the earlier of age 65 or the plan's normal retirement age; (2) a participant reaches the 10th anniversary of participation in the plan; or (3) a participant terminates his or her service with the employer.

Mandatory Distributions After Age 70½ or Retirement

Under Code Section 401(a)(9)(C), if an employee owns more than 5% of the company, the plan must begin distributing benefits to him or her by April 1 of the calendar year following the calendar year in which the employee attains age 70½. If an employee does not own more than 5% of the company, the plan must begin distributing benefits by April 1 of the calendar year following the later of (1) the calendar year in which the employee attains age 70½ or (2) the calendar year in which the employee retires.

Distributions After Death

Code Section 401(a)(9)(B) provides that if the participant dies *after* distributions have begun but before it has been completed, the remaining distributions must be given to the participant's beneficiary at least as rapidly as they would have been given to the participant. If the participant dies *before* distributions have begun, either (1) the entire benefit must be distributed within five years after the participant's death, or (2) distributions can be made in installments over the life or the life expectancy of the participant's beneficiary, starting within a year after the participant's death (however, if the beneficiary is the participant's surviving spouse, distributions need not begin until the date on which the participant would have reached age 70½).

How the Special ESOP Rules and Qualified Plan Rules Interact

When the ESOP rules and the general qualified plan rules interact, the rule that would produce an earlier distribution governs. In general, the ESOP rules tend to require distributions to be made earlier, so the interplay of the ESOP rules and the general qualified plan rules usually results in an earlier distribution than would be the case in a non-ESOP plan. For example, suppose that an ESOP's plan year is the calendar year and its normal retirement age is 65. Sally Jones retires in 2002 at age 65, having been in the plan for seven years (since 1995). Under the general qualified plan rules, she could have to wait until 2006, which is the year after the 10th anniversary of her participation in the plan, for distributions to begin. However, the special ESOP rules mandate that her distribution begin in 2003, the plan year following the plan year of her retirement.

Sometimes the general qualified plan rules require an earlier distribution than the ESOP rules would require. For example, suppose again that the ESOP's plan year is the calendar year and its normal retirement age is 65. Fred Smith, who has been in the ESOP for 15 years, quits in 2002 at the age of 64. Under the ESOP rules, Fred would potentially have to wait until the sixth year after that (2008) for benefit distribution to begin. However, the general qualified plan rules override the ESOP rules because when Fred reaches age 65 in 2003, the three conditions given above will all have occurred (age 65 or retirement age, 10th anniversary of participation, and termination of service). Therefore, Fred's distribution must start no later than the 60th day of 2004 (i.e., the 60th day after the plan year, 2003, in which the latest of those three events occurred).

Where the Special ESOP Rules Do Not Apply (Pre-1987 Stock)

Because the special ESOP rules in Code Section 409(o) do not apply (unless the plan otherwise provides) to distributions attributable to stock acquired before 1987, the general qualified plan rules control such distributions, which often has the effect of delaying them compared to distributions subject to the special ESOP rules. For example, take an ESOP that did a leveraged buyout of a company in 1986 and never acquired any more stock. The ESOP's normal retirement age is 65, and the plan specifies distributions will not take place before then. In 2002, Ann, a participant who has been in the ESOP since 1986, quits the company at age 40, and hopes to receive her distributions soon. Alas, she must wait until 2027 (i.e., the year in which she reaches 65) to start receiving distributions. Such distribution would need to commence no later than 60 days after the end of the 2027 plan year. If the ESOP deal took place in 1987, then the special ESOP rules would apply, and she would only have to wait until 2008. Also note that the company could amend its plan to allow pre-retirement distributions.

Distributions While Participants Are Still Employed

An ESOP is primarily a deferred income plan that provides employees with benefits after they terminate employment. However, in certain circumstances, participants may receive benefits from the ESOP while they are still employed:

- As discussed at the end of this chapter, participants may "diversify" their accounts after a certain period and may receive cash or stock directly (however, similarly to the special ESOP distribution rules, companies are not required to offer diversification for stock acquired before 1987).
- The employer may choose to pay dividends directly to participants on company stock allocated to their accounts.
- As noted above, 5%-or-more owners must begin to receive distributions when they reach age 70½.
- There are certain other circumstances in which the plan may provide for in-service distributions, such as after a fixed number of years, upon attainment of a specified age, or due to the participant's financial hardship.

Form of Distributions: Cash or Stock

An ESOP may provide that distributions will be in cash, stock, or a combination of cash and stock. Closely held companies often have concerns about former employees holding company stock, either due to matters such as selling it to third parties or, in S corporations, the possibility of either exceeding the 75-shareholder S corporation limit or having the employee transfer the shares to an ineligible S corporation owner.

ESOP participants generally have the right to demand a distribution in the form of whole shares of stock, with the value of any fractional share paid in cash (even for portions of their ESOP account that were held in cash) and can then sell that stock to anyone, except that the plan may provide that the employer and the ESOP have rights of first refusal to match any offer received from a third party for such stock.

However, if the employer is a closely held company whose charter or bylaws restrict the ownership of all or substantially all (although there is no authority for what constitutes "substantially all," it is generally believed to be at least 85%) of its stock to employees or a qualified plan, or if the employer is an S corporation, the ESOP is not required to distribute stock; instead, it can distribute cash, or the employer can require the employee to sell distributed stock back to the employer.

Buying the Stock Back from Employees

Closely held companies that sponsor an ESOP must provide a "put option" on company stock distributed to participants that allows them to demand that the company repurchase the stock at its current fair market value. At a minimum, the put option must be available during two periods, one for at least 60 days immediately following distribution and one for at least 60 days after the determination of the stock's fair market value during the following plan year. The repurchase obligation (also sometimes referred to as the "repurchase liability") that the put option creates is one of the main ongoing considerations in operating an ESOP.

The company may pay for repurchased shares in a single lump sum payment or in up to six annual installments over a period not exceeding five years (if adequate security is provided). The company's obligation to make the installment payments should be evidenced by a secured promissory note bearing interest at a reasonable rate. If the ESOP repurchases shares on an installment basis, the company must provide security and guarantee the ESOP's promissory note. Since the company can pay the employee in installments over a period of up to five years, selling the stock to the company does not mean the employee will immediately receive the full amount.

For public companies (those whose stock is readily tradable on an established market), there is no put option and no repurchase obligation. If employees of such companies receive stock instead of cash, they can simply sell it on the appropriate stock exchange any time they wish.

Participant Consent Requirement

Code Section 411(a)(11) and the regulations thereunder prohibit distributions being made without the participant's consent when the present value of the participant's benefit exceeds $5,000. The participant must be informed in writing of the right, if any, to defer receipt of the distribution, and must provide written consent only after receiving such information.

The consent requirement does not apply to dividend distributions that are deductible under Code Section 404(k) or to distributions after the death of the participant.

Employee Taxes

Participants pay no tax on stock allocated to their ESOP accounts until they receive distributions, at which time they are taxed on the distributions. If they are younger than age 59½ (or age 55 if they have terminated employment), they, like employees in qualified plans generally, are subject not only to applicable taxes but also to an additional 10% excise tax unless they roll the money over into an IRA or a qualified retirement plan maintained by another company (or unless the participant terminated employment due to death or disability). Employees born before 1936 who have participated in the plan for five years are eligible for favorable 10-year income averaging on lump-sum distributions.

If the money *is* rolled over into an IRA or another qualified retirement plan, the employee pays no tax until the money is withdrawn, at which point it is taxed as ordinary income.. A distribution from the ESOP is not eligible for rollover if it is one of a series of annual installments over a period of 10 years (or more), if it is a minimum required distribution after attainment of age 70½ (as described above), if it is a distribution made on account of a participant's hardship, or if it is a dividend that is paid directly to plan participants.

When dividends are directly paid to plan participants on the stock allocated to their ESOP accounts, such dividends are fully taxable, although they are exempt from income tax withholding and are not subject to the excise tax that applies to early distributions.

The Net Unrealized Appreciation Strategy

When participants receive a lump-sum distribution of stock after reaching age 59½ or terminating employment, they are not taxed, unless they so choose, on the net unrealized appreciation (NUA) of the shares—the appreciation in value of the stock while held by the plan, i.e., the difference between the amount the ESOP paid for the shares and the fair market value of the shares when they were distributed. Instead, they pay tax later, when they sell the shares. At that time, they are taxed at the long-term capital gains rates on the value of the shares when distributed, and at short- or long-term capital gains rates, as appropriate, for any appreciation in value that has occurred since distribution. (If this is the rare case in which employees make after-tax contributions to the plan, NUA is also excluded from income for non-lump sum distributions of stock attributable to the amounts they contributed.) The cost basis of the shares to the plan (or current fair market value, if lower), plus the cash distributed (if any), is taxed as ordinary income when received by the participant (except to the extent of a "rollover" to an IRA or qualified employee benefit plan). If a participant directs the "rollover" of the cash portion of his or her distribution and/or a portion of his or her share distribution, the shares of employer securities actually distributed (and not "rolled over") are eligible for the special NUA tax treatment, but the special NUA tax treatment is not available for any shares of employer securities that are "rolled over" to an IRA or an employee benefit plan.

In contrast, if the entire distribution is rolled over into an IRA (including if stock is put into an IRA and sold while in the IRA), it will be taxed as ordinary income when withdrawn. Thus, employees, especially those in high tax brackets, whose ESOP stock accounts include a great deal of NUA may be able to save a considerable amount in taxes by avoiding a rollover and employing the NUA strategy.

This strategy is not for everyone, however. First, if the company is closely held (as most ESOP companies are), will the company will buy back the stock? (Typically, the mandatory buyback period will have passed by the time the employee in this scenario finally sells the stock.) Second, even with a public company, what if the stock value falls between the date of distribution and the date the participant sells the stock? All the potential tax savings and more could be lost. In the end, the NUA strategy is mainly useful for employees of public companies who receive stock that has greatly appreciated in value (thus increasing the potential tax savings) and who are confident that their company's stock value will not fall before they sell the shares.

Withholding

If a distribution is eligible to be rolled over into an IRA or another qualified retirement plan but the participant does not elect a direct rollover, the company generally must withhold 20% for federal income tax from a distribution. Eligible rollover distributions do not include those, for example, that are paid as a life annuity; paid over a specified period of 10 years or more; payments of dividends directly distributed to participants; paid on account of a participant's hardship; or distributions paid because the participant reaches 70½ and is a 5% owner. Such distributions are subject to 10% federal income tax withholding unless the person receiving the distribution elects otherwise.

Withholding applies only to the immediately taxable portion of the distribution, not to net unrealized appreciation (discussed above). Thus, for a lump-sum distribution in stock and cash, the amount subject to withholding is (1) the amount distributed in cash plus (2) the lower of the ESOP's cost basis in the shares or the shares' current value.

There is an exception to the withholding rules: the amount withheld must not exceed the amount of cash distributed, so, for example, a distribution in stock is not subject to withholding. Also, as noted above, dividends paid directly to participants are not subject to withholding.

Diversification

Under Code Section 409(a)(28)(B), after ESOP participants reach age 55 and have participated in the plan for ten years, they have the right during the following five years to diversify up to a total of 25% of company stock that was acquired by the ESOP after December 31, 1986, and has been allocated to their accounts; during the sixth year, they may diversify up to a total of 50%, minus any previously diversified shares. A participant must be given a 90-day period to decide whether to diversify, and then the ESOP trustee has a further 90 days after the participant's 90-day period expires in which to implement the participant's request.

It is important to note that diversification is cumulative; that is, as a participant diversifies his or her account, the amount available for further diversification is diminished. For example, say that a participant starts off with 1,000 shares in the first year of diversification and diversifies 10%, or 100 shares, leaving 900 shares of company stock. In year two, 100 more shares are allocated to the participant's account, for a total of 1,000 shares. At this time, to compute the 25% available for diversification, the 100 previously diversified shares are added to the 1,000 undiversified shares, for a total of 1,100 shares. The *cumulative* amount available for diversification at this point is 275 shares (25% of 1,100), but the 100 shares previously diversified are subtracted from this, leaving 175 shares (out of the 1,000) that can be diversified.

To satisfy the diversification requirement, the ESOP may offer at least three alternative investments (other than company stock) within the ESOP, offer a transfer to a another qualified plan, such as a 401(k) plan, that offers three or more investment alternatives (other than company stock), distribute cash to the participants, or distribute stock to the participants. Remember that in a closely held company, a stock distribution will be subject to the requirement that the company must offer to repurchase the shares at the then-current fair market value. Also, employees who have not attained age 59½ will be subject to the 10% excise tax on early distributions (in addition to regular income tax) if they diversify by taking a distribution of either cash or stock. A participant does not have the right to demand that a diversification distribution be made in the form of company stock (i.e., the ESOP could provide for only cash diversification distributions).

The above requirements (i.e., 25% and then 50% over the course of six years starting at age 55 with ten years in the plan) are the legal minimums: the ESOP plan document may be drafted to allow participants to diversify more than these minimum percentages and/or at a younger age. However, if the ESOP allows participants to diversify above the legal minimums, they have the right to demand that the "extra" amounts be paid out in company stock (subject to the restrictions discussed above), although this is unlikely to be an issue. In addition, the "extra" amounts cannot be taken into account when determining whether the diversification requirements have been satisfied.

There are two exceptions to the diversification requirement. First, if the value of the participant's ESOP stock account is less than $500, the company may, but need not, offer the participant the opportunity to diversify his or her account. Second, shares acquired by the ESOP before 1987 are not subject to diversification (but again, the company may choose to include them as well).

CHAPTER 10

Questions and Answers on Operating an ESOP

Corey Rosen

Who's In the Plan?

Q. Who has to participate in an ESOP?

The rules for participation in an ESOP are the same as for other qualified employee benefit plans (pensions, profit sharing, etc.). The rules provide several tests to assure plans meet minimum anti-discrimination requirements. Virtually all ESOP companies, however, cover at least all full-time employees (1,000 hours of service or more in a year) 21 years of age or older with at least one year of service. Employees covered by a collective bargaining agreement can be excluded from coverage, provided the company bargains in good faith about whether they should be included. These are minimum requirements; companies can include more employees (such as including part-time people or more recent hires).

The law does provide some additional exceptions. For instance, the ESOP can include only employees in a separate line of business, such as a division or subsidiary, that has 50 or more employees. This will not apply, however, if the intent is to circumvent the coverage rules. For instance, a plan could not just cover a division set up of management people and exclude a division that has only non-management employees.

An alternative approach provides three tests for coverage. To use this approach, a company applies percentage tests to at least a minimum employee group. This group must include all employees 21 or older who have completed at least 1,000 hours of service in a plan year, but can exclude nonresident aliens, employees in a separate line of business with 50 or more employees, and employees covered by a collective bargaining agreement. The percentage tests are as follows:

1. At least 70% of non-highly compensated employees must be covered, or

2. The percentage of non-highly compensated employees who are covered is at least 70% of the percentage of highly compensated covered, or

3. There is a classification system that does not discriminate in favor of highly compensated employees, and the average benefit percentage (generally, the percentage contributed to the plan) for the covered non-highly compensated group is at least 70% of that contributed to the covered highly compensated group.

Although these alternative tests are available, they are very rarely used in ESOPs. The kind of exclusion the rules provide is contrary to the spirit most ESOP companies are trying to set up and may also cause practical problems, as noted below.

Allocating ESOP Shares

Q. How is stock allocated in an ESOP?

Most companies allocate stock based on W-2 compensation, plus elective deferrals under Section 401(k) plans and cafeteria plans. That is, each participant in the plan gets a percentage of the total shares allocated equal to that participant's percentage of total eligible pay. Eligible pay excludes pay in excess of $200,000 in 2002 (to be indexed for inflation in $5,000 increments after that). While W-2 compensation is the norm, compensation could also be defined to exclude bonuses or other "add-ons" to pay, provided the effect is not to push allocations toward more highly paid people. About two-thirds of all ESOPs allocate based on relative pay. Alternatively, companies might:

1. Allocate the same amount to everyone;

2. Use relative pay, but with a lower cap on what pay can be included;

3. Give points for seniority; or

4. Make the contributions based on what employees defer to a 401(k) plan.

In all but the 401(k) plan formula, however, the plan must be written to provide a "fail-safe" to assure that no single "highly compensated employee" (this is a term defined by law) will get more than what would have been allocated based on a straight pay formula.

These alternative formulas could limit how much an employer could contribute to an ESOP, however, because the maximum contribution is 25% of *eligible* pay, and all of these formulas limit eligible pay more than what would be eligible under a relative pay formula.

Q. How is stock released from an ESOP suspense account for allocations to participants?

Each year, as the loan is repaid, a percentage of shares held in the ESOP trust equal to the percentage of the loan that has been repaid that year is released from what is called "the ESOP suspense account." The shares are then allocated to employee participant accounts.

The company can use one of two formulas, the "principal-only" method or the "principal and interest method." The principal-only method releases a percentage of the shares that is equal to the percentage of the total principal paid. This method cannot be used unless the payments of principal and interest on the loan are no less rapid than level annual payments of principal and interest over a 10-year loan, using standard amortization tables to determine allowable interest rates.

The principal and interest method releases shares based on a formula. The number of shares held in the suspense account just before the release is multiplied by a fraction, the numerator of which is the principal and interest payments for the year and the denominator of which is the principal and interest payments remaining on the loan, including the current year. In other words, shares are allocated based on the total amount of the remaining loan (principal and interest) paid that year. The number of years on the loan must be fixed, not variable; renewal or extensions of the loan cannot be considered; and the interest rate is the rate that applies at the end of the year involved.

The principal-only method releases shares more slowly, in most cases, and is often preferred by banks.

Q. How do ESOP allocations interact with limits for other benefit plans?

For plan years starting after December 31, 2001, companies can make tax-deductible contributions of up to 25% of the aggregate eligible pay of employees in the plan (or plans), regardless of whether the ESOP is leveraged or not or is in a C or S corporation. In C corporation ESOPs, reasonable dividends that are used to repay a loan, are passed through to participants, or are reinvested by participants in company stock in the ESOP do not count toward the 25% limit. Eligible pay is defined to include employee deferrals into 401(k) plans or cafeteria plans. This limit applies to the total amount of a company's contributions to its defined contribution plans (ESOPs, stock bonus plans, profit sharing plans, and 401(k) plans); contributions to defined benefit plans do not count toward this limit.

The maximum "annual addition" to any one individual's account under the plans cannot exceed the lesser of 100% of pay or $40,000 in 2002 (to be indexed for inflation). In C corporation ESOPs, dividends that are used to repay a loan, are passed through to participants, or are reinvested by participants in company stock in the ESOP do not count toward the 100% of pay or maximum dollar limit. Employee deferrals do count toward the 100% of pay or maximum dollar limitation. Annual additions thus include all employer and employee contributions to defined contribution plans. In S corporations, interest payments and forfeitures count toward the maximum annual addition limits, and interest payments count toward the 25% of pay maximum deductible employer contribution.

C corporations can go beyond the 25% limit, however, by paying "reasonable" dividends on the ESOP shares. These dividends are normally paid on all shares, allocated and unallocated. (Dividends can also be passed through directly to participants, but doing so does not raise the contribution limit because dividends are paid to employees, not the plan.) "Reasonable" has never been legally defined, but most practitioners believe it means within the range paid on comparable classes of stock in similar companies, must be capable of being paid regularly, and must not result in unreasonable compensation. The dividends must be included in alternative minimum tax calculations.

Vesting Rules
Q. What are the vesting rules for ESOPs?

Generally, employees must vest (earn a non-forfeitable right to their account balances) according to one of two schedules, or faster. One approach (cliff vesting) allows no vesting for the first five years of service, then 100% vesting at the end of the fifth year. A second allows graduated vesting to begin at 20% after the third year and increase 20% per year thereafter. Faster vesting is allowed. Faster vesting schedules are required if plans are "top heavy," meaning more than 60% of the allocated benefits go to key employees as defined by the law.

However, if the ESOP is being used to provide a match to a 401(k) plan, there are special exceptions. If the company is using the safe harbor matching contribution rule that allows companies to avoid anti-discrimination testing by making minimum contributions to the 401(k) plan, then contributions must vest immediately. These safe harbor rules allow a company to avoid testing if it contributes at least 3% of pay to all participants (regardless of what they defer) or a 100% match for the first 3% that employees defer and a 50% match for deferrals between 3% and 5% of pay. In that case, these contributions must vest immediately. For plan years starting after December 31, 2001, this safe harbor vesting rule still applies, but any matching contributions (including those made as part of an ESOP/401(k) contribution) must vest on a faster schedule. They either must fully vest after three years of service (cliff vesting) or start at not less than 20% per year after the second year of service and continue until 100% vesting is reached after six years.

Q. Do prior years of service before an ESOP is set up count toward vesting?

Prior years of service do not have to count, unless the ESOP replaces a previous plan within five years, in which case prior service must be counted. Companies can, however, count prior years (and most do), or give partial credit for prior years.

ESOP Distribution Rules

Q. When does a company have to start distributing an employee's account?

If an employee leaves because of death, retirement, or disability, or reaches retirement age after termination but before an ESOP payout has started, distributions must start during the plan year following the event, unless the participant elects otherwise. Otherwise, distribution must start within six years after the plan year of termination, unless the participant elects otherwise or there is an outstanding ESOP loan, in which case distributions to terminating employees do not have to start until the loan is repaid. As noted below, this does not apply in the same way to employees receiving distributions because of death or retirement, and, in any event, distributions for any 5% owners must begin not later than April 1 following the calendar year in which a participant reaches age 70½. Once the distribution commences, it can be paid out in a lump sum or in equal installments, with interest, over a period not exceeding five years (or more for balances over $800,000 as of 2002, indexed annually for inflation).

Q. A company can defer the start of its ESOP distributions until after its loan is repaid. Does this apply in death, retirement, or disability?

First, note that this exception applies only to shares acquired by an ESOP loan. Distributions for other shares (including any shares for which the loan has been paid) must follow the rules above. In the case of death, for shares on which the loan has not yet been repaid, distribution does not have to start right away, but it must be made to the beneficiary and completed within five years, regardless of the loan status. For retirement, distribution must start no later than the 60th day after the end of the plan year in which the later of these events occur: (1) the participant reaches age 65 or, if earlier, the plan's normal retirement age, (2) departure at normal retirement age, or (3) the 10th anniversary of participation in the plan for employees who have separated from service.

This means that employees who reach age 65 prior to 10 years from the anniversary date of their original participation in the plan (note this is not 10 years' service, but 10 years from the start of participation) could have to wait until the 10th anniversary to become eligible. Plan participation would include years in a predecessor defined contribution plan if it were not terminated but rather were folded into the ESOP.

While this delay is allowed by the law, that does not mean it will be in the plan document. Many plan documents provide for earlier payouts for retirees. Alternatively, many other plans provide for the maximum legal flexibility but, in practice, pay out sooner. From an employee relations standpoint, not to mention the need of employees for retirement income, this earlier distribution policy normally makes sense.

Q. Can a company require employees to take cash instead of shares?

Yes, if (1) either (a) company bylaws specify that all or substantially all the stock in the company be owned by employees or (b) the company is an S corporation, and (2) the plan document specifies that the company can offer the cash value of accounts instead. If the company is a bank and has a cash-only provision, it can also choose not to offer employees shares when they leave.

Q. In an ESOP, if the company cannot require employees to take cash for the shares, does it have a right of first refusal on shares distributed to former employees?

Yes, if the plan so provides.

Q. What is the employee's tax liability for the distribution?

If the employee puts the money into an IRA or the distribution is rolled into another qualified plan in another company (this would be unusual except in the case where an ESOP company is purchased by another company), there is no tax liability until the money is withdrawn, when the withdrawal is taxed as ordinary income. Otherwise, the employee must pay ordinary income tax on the value of company contributions to the plan, capital gains taxes on the appreciation in share value when sold (this only applies to lump-sum distributions), and a 10% penalty if the distribution is not for death, termination after age 55, or disability.

For capital gains holding period requirement purposes, the time the shares have been in the employee's account do count.

The rollover to an IRA or another qualified plan is normally done as a direct rollover, meaning the employee notifies the company that the allocation should be rolled over into the successor plan before the allocation is paid out. Alternatively, the amount can be paid out to the employee, who then has 60 days to roll it into an IRA. However, in making this choice, companies need to consider the possible impact of withholding plan rules.

The ESOP Committee

Q. What is the ESOP Committee?

An ESOP Committee is usually appointed by the board of directors and delegated the responsibility to oversee day-to-day operations of the plan. It is often called the ESOP Administration Committee or Plan Administration Committee.

Q. Does every ESOP company have to have an ESOP Committee?

No. All ESOPs must have a trustee and someone to administer the plan, but there is no legal requirement for there to be an ESOP Committee. In practice, however, plan documents almost always specify that there be an ESOP Committee to administer the plan and oversee its operations.

Q. Is the ESOP Committee the same as the plan fiduciary or the plan trustee?

A plan fiduciary is the person or body that makes decisions affecting the plan. ESOPs have named fiduciaries, who can be anyone or any group (the board, the trustee, management, the ESOP Committee, all individual plan participants, or anyone else). Just because the plan names a fiduciary, however, does not mean that someone else cannot act as a fiduciary by making a decision for the operation of the plan. An ESOP Committee can both be named as a fiduciary and act as a fiduciary even if it is not so named. It can also serve as the plan trustee. The ESOP Committee, however, could play neither role if it does not make decisions, but simply renders advice, to the fiduciary and/or trustee.

Q. What does the ESOP Committee typically do?

ESOP Committees can have several responsibilities. They may be responsible for plan design, including recommending plan amendments to the board. In some cases, this could involve fiduciary issues, such as changing the plan in a way that reduces promised benefits to participants beyond what is allowed by specific ESOP exceptions to ERISA. They also can make fiduciary decisions for the plan directly or by directing the trustee of the plan to make the decision. Alternatively, they can just have an advisory role to the fiduciaries. They often assume responsibility for administrative oversight of the plan (making sure that statements go out, that participants are paid, that allocations are properly made, etc.), although they rarely actually do the administration. Finally, they often act as the vehicle for communicating the plan to participants and even overseeing the company's employee involvement program.

Q. What would be examples of fiduciary decisions the ESOP Committee might make?

Fiduciary decisions would include, but not be limited to, making decisions as to the voting of shares in the ESOP where the law does not require a pass-through of voting rights to participants, making decisions about investing plan assets both in employer stock and other investments, selling stock, assuring that the ESOP pays no more than fair market value, selecting qualified advisors, assuring that the operation and design of the plan comply with ERISA, and moving assets from the ESOP to another plan. The committee may implement these decisions itself or direct the trustee to carry them out.

By contrast, recommending to the board of directors that the plan be changed or even terminated, voting on candidates for the board, and performing the normal administration of the plan, presuming it is done in compliance with the law, are all examples of things that are not normally fiduciary acts.

Q. How are ESOP Committee members chosen?

Because many of the functions of the committee are inherently duties of the board that are delegated to the committee, most ESOP Committees are appointed by the board. Other than general legal and fiduciary concerns, however, there are no rules about who can be on the ESOP Committee or how they should be selected. In many companies, the committee consists of members of management and/or the board; in some, it is just a single member of management. More participative companies get non-management employees involved on the committee, as minority or majority members. Usually these employees are elected by other employees, but sometimes they are appointed by management or are volunteers.

Voting Rights

Q. Who actually votes the ESOP shares?

The plan's trustee generally votes all the shares in the ESOP, whether allocated or not. The plan document indicates how the trustee decides how to vote. In closely held companies, the trustee must follow participant directions on allocated shares on several major corporate issues (sale, liquidation, recapitalization, merger, and related issues), but does not have to solicit instructions on voting for the board, agreeing to tender the stock, or the sale of assets, among other issues. In publicly traded companies, trustees must follow participant directions on allocated shares on all issues presented for a shareholder vote. Otherwise, the trustee usually follows the directions of management, the plan committee, or another entity specified in the plan. While this usually causes no problems, the trustee, or the person(s) directing the trustee, is still responsible to act in the best interests of plan participants. Note that while the law requires trustees to solicit employee instructions on specified issues, the trustee has a higher legal obligation under ERISA to override these instructions if they are contrary to the law or plan documents. Such an action would be very rare and would need compelling justification, however.

Q. Who actually has control in an ESOP?

In a publicly traded company, the board of directors is elected by all the shareholders and is responsible for the hiring and firing of management. Employees in a public company ESOP can vote their allocated shares just like any other shareholder. In some public companies, they can direct the voting of unallocated shares as well. In practice, however, employees rarely use the vote any more actively than do other individual shareholders, meaning an ESOP has little or no impact on day-to-day operations of the company or the composition of its board.

In a closely held company, there is more variation. In the most common scenario, employees have only limited voting rights, and these do not include voting for the board. Instead, the trustee exercises voting rights. Typically, the trustee is selected by either the board of directors or management. The trustee can be anyone, but is usually either a corporate officer or, in larger companies, a outsider, such as a bank. The trustee, in turn, votes the ESOP shares for the election of the board. Usually, the trustee acts according to directions from the ESOP Committee. The Committee is usually appointed by management or the board and is made up of company officers. This circular arrangement means, in effect, that management and/or the board (and these are often the same) controls the company in much the same way it did prior to the ESOP. Of course, whoever acts as an ESOP's fiduciary (that is, whoever makes decisions for the plan) is legally responsible to make those interests in the best interests of plan participants.

While companies have the discretion to set up the plan this way, more and more plans provide for greater employee involvement. For instance, there may be non-management employee representation on the ESOP Committee. Employees may be given full voting rights on their shares. Employees may also elect one or more representatives to the board. Companies have found that this higher level of employee involvement is usually a plus for the company and very, very rarely results in significant policy changes other than ones on which there is consensus among the management group as well.

Trustee and Fiduciary Issues
Q. What is an ESOP trustee?

A trustee is the person or institution who normally has the formal responsibility to make sure the plan is operated for "the exclusive benefit of plan participants." Trustees can be "independent" or "directed." An independent trustee makes decisions for the plan based on the trustee's judgment, relying as needed on advice from qualified professionals; a directed trustee makes decisions based on the direction of another party, which could be the ESOP Committee, management, or employee participants (such as when employees direct the voting of their allocated shares). Directed trustees have very limited fiduciary responsibility, as explained below.

Q. Is the trustee the same as the fiduciary of an employee ownership plan?

In most cases, the trustee is the fiduciary, but the two functions are not necessarily the same. Plans must designate who is the fiduciary; they can designate this for all issues or have different fiduciaries for particular issues. A fiduciary is anyone who makes decisions about plan operations, including its management or the disposition of its assets. Fiduciaries can also be people who render investment advice for a fee. Thus, a directed trustee is not acting as a fiduciary because it is not making the decision. (Nonetheless, a directed trustee still must confirm that any directions received are consistent with the plan documents and ERISA; if they are not, the trustee should inform the fiduciary and work to create a decision that complies with these guidelines). Similarly, on any particular issue, the trustee may cede decision-making to someone else or share it with someone else. It is important to recognize that even though someone may not be named as a fiduciary, that person could act as a fiduciary, and have the legal responsibility of a fiduciary, by effectively making a decision with regard to plan operations that comes under fiduciary responsibilities.

Q. What kinds of decisions are fiduciary decisions?

There are many possible fiduciary decisions. First, we can exclude things that are not fiduciary duties. These include preparing reports to the government and employees, overseeing allocation, vesting, benefit distributions, and other "ministerial" functions, calculating and explaining benefits, processing claims, and other record-keeping tasks. Specific fiduciary duties do include the following:

1. Buying and selling plan assets, including employer stock.
2. Hiring qualified advisers.

3.   Determining that the ESOP is paying no more than fair market value.

4.   Assuring that the plan is operated in accordance with plan documents and ERISA; if the two conflict, ERISA rules govern.

5.   Making sure the terms of any ESOP loan are reasonable.

6.   Voting and/or directing the tendering of shares in the trust for which plan and ERISA rules do not require pass-through voting.

7.   Deciding whether to follow participant voting or tendering directions on unallocated or undirected shares.

8.   Responding to legitimate offers to purchase the company.

9.   Acting to protect plan interests with respect to corporate actions that could harm the interests of plan participants. See the following question for more detail on this issue.

Number 4 of these duties, assuring that the plan is operated in accordance with plan documents and ERISA, is very broad. It can include a variety of decisions. For instance, a fiduciary could be sued for failing to allow employees to vote their shares on required issues, for not giving employees appropriate information to make a decision when they vote, for failing to distribute benefits according to plan rules, for acting in a discriminatory manner in honoring the put option, for failing to assure the filing of reports so that the plan loses its qualified status, etc.

In general, fiduciaries must act according to the "prudent person" standard, "with the care, skill, prudence, and diligence under the circumstances then prevailing that a prudent man acting in a like capacity and familiar with such matters would use in the conduct of an enterprise of like character and with like aims." Fiduciaries must act for the "exclusive benefit of plan participants," meaning when there is a conflict between participant and other interests, participant interests, as defined by their investment interest in the plan, must be favored.

Q. Does the ESOP fiduciary have a role with respect to normal business operations as opposed to ERISA and plan document issues?

The trustee is the shareholder of record for corporate law purposes. As a fiduciary for these shares (or as directed by the entity or person acting as fiduciary), the trustee has all the rights any other shareholder would. These rights vary from state to state because as corporate law is a state law issue. They include such things as voting for board members, receiving corporate information, being notified of shareholder meetings, being able to vote for fundamental changes in the corporation, and protection against unfair diminution of value (such as buying out other shareholders with comparable ownership interests at a higher price).

There is no body of law, however, even suggesting just how the trustee/fiduciary should exercise these rights beyond the very minimal requirements of the law. While the trustee/fiduciary clearly could become a very active shareholder, it is not clear if there is a requirement to do so and, if so, under what circumstances. For instance, if the trustee/fiduciary knows management is self-dealing or making very poor decisions, should it intervene? Does it have an obligation to intervene? The Department of Labor has issued guidelines for all ERISA fiduciaries indicating that they have an obligation to review broad corporate operations, such as the composition of the board, appropriate personnel practices, and general strategic decisions, but these guidelines have not yet been tested in court with respect to ESOPs.

Q. What happens if a fiduciary violates fiduciary obligations?

The fiduciary can be sued, and is personally responsible for any losses that result.

Q. Can the fiduciary be indemnified or insured?

Companies can indemnify the fiduciary (promise to pay the costs of any judgments), but this could persuade a court that the company is ultimately the fiduciary. Fiduciaries can and should obtain fiduciary liability insurance, which the company may purchase.

Accounting Issues

Q. What is the accounting procedure for non-leveraged ESOPs?

If the company contributes new shares of stock, the value of the shares at the time of the contribution is counted as a compensation expense.

The par value of the shares is credited to common stock par value, while paid-in capital is credited at the difference between par value and current fair market value.

If the contribution is in cash and used to buy existing shares, the value of the contribution is charged to compensation expense, while cash is credited with the value of the contribution.

Footnote disclosures in either case should identify the plan and the employee groups covered, describe the company's contribution policy, and identify how much was contributed and when.

Q. How does the ESOP debt affect assets on the balance sheet?

On the asset side, there may be an increase in cash or other assets resulting from the ESOP's purchase of new shares, with the money from this purchase going toward some corporate purpose. This would not be the case if the ESOP is used to buy stock from an existing shareholder. The assets of the plan, however, are not reported as assets of the plan sponsor, nor is a note receivable from the plan should the plan sponsor be lending money to the ESOP. The plan sponsor, however, must show the issuance of shares, or the sale of treasury shares, to the ESOP on its balance sheet.

Q. What is the impact of the ESOP debt on the liabilities side of the balance sheet?

All ESOP debt, regardless of whether the company guarantees it or not, shows up as debt of the sponsor. (Note: this does not apply to ESOP loans made before June 19, 1989; for these plans, the debt does not show up as the sponsor's debt if the sponsor does not have an actual or implied commitment to repay the debt, although this is something that virtually every ESOP sponsor would have.)

Q. How does the ESOP debt affect the equity portion of the company's balance sheet?

When the debt is recorded on the balance sheet, an equal and offsetting debit is recorded in the equity section as a "contra equity account."

It has to appear here because the ESOP loan does not show up as an asset in the asset section. This contra equity account is eliminated as the ESOP debt is repaid. The amount of the release is equal to the number of shares released from the ESOP suspense account and allocated to participants. Because of the way this process works, the amount the contra equity account is reduced will not necessarily equal the amount that the debt is reduced.

The measure used for compensation cost in making these calculations varies with whether the company is using the principal only or principal and interest method for releasing shares. See the question on the income statement for more detail.

Q. How do dividends paid in a leveraged ESOP affect retained earnings?

Dividends paid on allocated ESOP stock are charged to retained earnings (except in the very rare case of dividends paid in certain transactions resulting from terminations of defined benefit plans). For dividends paid on unallocated stock to repay a loan, they are charged as compensation on the income statement.

Q. How is the contribution to the ESOP measured on the income statement?

Employer contributions to repay an ESOP loan are counted as compensation expense and repayment of interest. The repayment of interest is measured as it would be for any other loan. Compensation expense is more complicated. At its simplest, compensation expense would equal the amount of principal paid on the loan in any year. However, ESOP sponsors can also allocate shares using the principal plus interest method (see above, "Allocating ESOP Shares"). This has resulted in loans structured with unusual amortization schedules. Then, in 1987, Congress allowed companies to use dividends to repay loans, creating another layer of complexity. So starting in 1989, a new formula was required:

(Shares allocated for the period/total shares purchased)
x Original Principal + Interest Expense - Dividends

The value of the shares released from the ESOP suspense account, not the cost basis of the shares, is the value used for making these determinations.

CHAPTER 11

Things to Do with an ESOP Besides Buying Out the Owner

Corey Rosen

The most typical use of an ESOP is to provide a market for the shares of owners who want to sell all or part of their ownership interests. ESOPs are by no means limited to this application, however. They also can be used simply as an employee benefit plan, as a match to a 401(k) plan, to acquire new capital or other companies, to buy out a division of a company, to support the market for a thinly traded company's stock, or even, in a few select situations, to save a company that would otherwise close. This chapter looks at these other uses.

The ESOP As an Employee Benefit Plan

In many ESOP companies, the plan's purpose is simply to provide an incentive for employees linked to the company's performance. This kind of ESOP is conceptually and practically straightforward. The company typically will issue additional shares to contribute to the plan. These new shares dilute the interests of existing shareholders but also generate a tax deduction for the company equal to the fair market value of the stock contributed. Shares contributed to the plan are allocated to accounts for employees in the plan as they are contributed. Like other ESOP shares, they must be repurchased after employees terminate or retire.

In setting up a plan like this, companies must consider several issues. First, the issue of dilution must be faced. The simplest way to deal with this is to set an acceptable ceiling on dilution. For instance, assume the owners agree that they can accept a 25% dilution. When this figure is approached, the company can limit future stock contributions to shares that are repurchased from departing employees. That way, the plan would always maintain a 25% level of ownership. If this level of contribution seems inadequate to meet the overall target levels for employee retirement benefits, then additional cash can be contributed to the plan so long as the plan retains most of its investment in company stock.

While this is the simplest approach, it may not be the best one in terms of employee incentives because it limits what can go into the plan to an arbitrary number. A more dynamic approach would be to look at what the company wants to contribute to the plan on a percentage of pay basis. In most companies with an ESOP used as an incentive plan, there is both an ESOP and a 401(k) plan. Employees can defer pay into the 401(k) plan, and the company may make an additional cash match. The company also contributes a fixed percentage of pay to the ESOP each year, based on a determination of what overall percentage of pay the company should be contributing to the ESOP and 401(k) plan to attract, retain, and motivate employees. In this model, dilution becomes a function of compensation needs. Moreover, as payroll grows, dilution will grow as well. Owners may find that acceptable, however, because the growth usually implies that they now own a smaller piece of a bigger company.

A third approach is to make the determination of how much goes into the ESOP based on profitability or some other performance target. For example, the company might put a percentage of pretax profits into the plan each year. Usually, this percentage is calculated using one of two ways. The first method is to provide an amount that in a normal year the company would consider appropriate and meaningful. The second method is to provide an amount based on an assessment of what seems like an affordable and reasonable percentage of profits to set aside for employees. Here too, the dilution of other owners will vary. However, because the amount going to employees grows only if the company's profits grow, it is even clearer that the owners will own a smaller part of a larger company.

Whatever approach is chosen, some key issues need to be kept in mind. First, for plans years in 2002 and later, the maximum deductible contribution to the ESOP and other defined contribution plans (401(k), profit sharing, stock bonus, and money purchase plans) is 25% of the eligible pay of plan participants. Unlike prior years, employee deferrals into the 401(k) plan do not add into this calculation. Second, contributions have to be more than symbolic. While research cannot pinpoint a dividing line and say "more than this is enough, and less than this does not work," the average contribution to an ESOP of this type is in the range of 5% to 10% of pay, with many plans above this amount. Third, if the plan is to work as an incentive, employees need to know what they need to do to earn it (if there is a profit sharing formula that triggers it) and what makes the stock price go up and down. As in all ESOP companies, a management style that shares financial information regularly and allows employees structured opportunities to share ideas and information can help achieve this goal.

If the company is an S corporation, another consideration is the required distributions that must be made to the ESOP. Like any other owner, the ESOP must receive a pro-rata share of any distributions. So if the 75% owners get $150,000, the ESOP, with its 25%, must get $50,000. This is not considered a contribution to the ESOP but rather earnings on ESOP shares. The distribution would be allocated to employees based on their account values. This additional contribution could be used to buy additional company shares, buy back shares from departing employees, or simply as an additional cash contribution to employees. However it is used, it adds to employee accounts and reduces corporate cash flow. In many cases, this will be completely acceptable; in others it will present a serious issue.

An ESOP used as an incentive plan may also be the basis for a subsequent purchase of shares by the plan. A plan might operate primarily as an incentive for several years or more before one or more owners wants to sell. At that point, there will be an established plan with a history of valuations and a base of ownership that will make it easy to get to the 30% ownership level required for the tax-deferred sale available to owners in C corporation ESOPs.

Using the ESOP to Match 401(k) Plan Contributions

Because 401(k) plans require minimum participation levels, companies often match employee payroll deferrals (typically at 25% to 75% of the contribution). The match can be in any number of investment assets the company chooses, including company stock. One way to provide this match is with an ESOP. The ESOP and 401(k) plan can be integrated into a single plan document or can operate side-by-side. The latter approach is administratively more flexible, although it requires two separate plan documents to be drawn up.

In the simplest approach, the company just contributes stock or cash to buy stock to a nonleveraged ESOP. The contribution may be based on what employees defer, on company profits, or a straight percentage of pay formula. In a more sophisticated approach, the company sets up a leveraged ESOP that borrows money to acquire shares. The allocation of stock from the leveraged ESOP is used to determine the match. For instance, say employees are putting $1 million into the 401(k) from their own deferrals. A leveraged ESOP might acquire 100,000 shares at $20 per share with a 10-year loan and repay 10% of the principal each year. Stock with an original cost of $200,000 per year and $20 per share per year would then be allocated as an employee match in the first year.

But now say that in year two, the stock is worth $25 per share. Now $250,000 in stock value will be released to employee accounts. If a few years later the stock goes to $50 per share, then $500,000 would be released. Unless payroll deferrals have grown as quickly, employees will be getting a larger match to their 401(k) accounts. The actual cost to the employer will be the same $20 per share, and the amount of the contribution the company records for purposes of contribution limits will also be $20 per share. Accounting rules stipulate that the value declared for the income statement, however, will be the value of the shares when released.

Because the value of the match would vary from year to year with the stock price, the company needs to make some choices about how the match will be made. One way to do this would be to allow the matching amount to vary with the value of the shares. If the share value rose quickly, as happened in many 401(k)/ESOP combinations in the 1990s, employees would see very large matches. If it dropped, the matching amount would fall. Another approach would be to borrow only enough money so that the repayment of principal would release what would normally be expected to be a part of the matching requirement and "top off" the remainder with cash.

Whether the match is leveraged or nonleveraged, the employer needs to decide whether the contribution should literally be a match to what employees defer or just should be a straight contribution. A straight contribution of 3% of pay or more, regardless of how much, if anything, employees defer, has the advantage of automatically qualifying the plan as meeting the testing rules for the 401(k) plan. Aside from solving the discrimination problems, it makes sure everyone gets at least some ownership. By contrast, a match-only approach means stock just goes to those who make wage deferrals, and goes more to those who defer more. Of course, the employer may want to use the ESOP contribution to encourage 401(k) deferrals, in which case this outcome would be precisely what is desired. In some cases, a middle ground will be chosen with a 3% base contribution and the remainder made as an actual match.

Where stock is publicly traded, companies also need to decide if employees should be allowed to move stock matches to other investments. At least some employees will want to do this, and it may make good financial sense for them to do so. But will this mean too little stock will be retained in the plan? Closely held companies will rarely want to allow employees to make these choices because it would require compliance with securities laws.

One wrinkle of an ESOP/401(k) plan is that companies using the safe harbor matching contribution rule that allows companies to avoid anti-discrimination testing by making minimum contributions to the 401(k) plan must vest the contributions immediately. For plan years starting after December 31, 2001, this safe harbor vesting rule still applies, plus all matching contributions must vest on a faster schedule. They either must fully vest after three years of service (cliff vesting) or start at not less than 20% per year after the second year of service and continue until 100% vesting is reached after six years (graded vesting).

Finally, an ESOP/401(k) plan makes it possible for employees to reinvest any dividends paid to them on company stock in a very tax-efficient way. For plan years in 2002 and later, dividends employees voluntarily reinvest in company stock are tax-deductible to the employer. While these dividends are normally taxable to the employee, the company can create a dividend switchback program that can provide the equivalent of a pretax dividend. In this approach, the employer designates the payroll department to receive the dividend. The employee has an amount of pay equivalent to the amount of the dividend deferred into a 401(k) plan, and the payroll department increases the amount paid out as salary to the employee by the same amount. This procedure has been approved in numerous private letter rulings.

Using an ESOP to Acquire New Capital of Other Companies

When Louis Kelso created the ESOP back in the 1950s, his vision was that companies would use it to finance new capital. They would borrow money to buy machinery, buildings, land, and other productive assets that would pay for themselves in extra corporate earnings. By financing the loan through an ESOP, employees would share in the additional ownership value this capital created.

In practice, this has been used less often than Kelso hoped, but it is an important part of many ESOP companies' strategies. Say that a printing company wants to buy a new $500,000 press. Normally, it would borrow the money and deduct the interest. With an ESOP, it would have the ESOP borrow the money (technically, the loan would usually go to the company, which would relend it to the ESOP). The ESOP would use the $500,000 loan to buy new shares in the company, and the company would use the $500,000 to buy the press. The company would then repay the loan by making tax-deductible contributions to the ESOP, thus deducting both principal and interest. As the loan was repaid, shares would be allocated to employee accounts. Other owners would suffer a dilution in terms of the percentage of the company they owned, but if the press proved to be a good investment, the company would gain at least as much in value as was invested (here, $500,000), so the value of their stock would not be any lower, and it could be higher thanks to the tax break and possible additional employee productivity.

Given these advantages, why don't more companies finance capital acquisitions this way? The principal explanation, of course, is that owners would rather keep ownership to themselves. Even though the ESOP could save them some tax money, the tax savings pay for only part of the cost of giving up ownership of the asset. Additional productivity gains are only possible, not guaranteed, and may not make up the difference not accounted for by the tax savings. On the other hand, if a company wants to share ownership anyway, or, especially, if it is already primarily ESOP-owned, then financing capital acquisitions this way can be very attractive.

Buying capital is one way to expand. Buying entire companies is another. The same leveraged approach described above would work to buy another company. But what if the acquiring company is a closely held company that already has an ESOP? Can the acquirer get the owners of the target company the tax deferral advantage available to other sellers to ESOPs in C corporations?

The answer is that it is possible, but requires several extra steps to be taken. In order to qualify the seller for the tax deferral, a few general criteria must be met:

1. The stock in the acquirer must have been held for at least three years. The owner of the target company must have held the securities he or she is selling to the ESOP (or other securities that qualify through "tacking" provisions that treat them as equivalent, such as ownership of preferred shares converted to common in the same company or partnership interests that have been converted to shares in a C corporation) for at least three years before the transaction.

2. The acquiring company must be a C corporation.

3. The transaction will need to meet the rules of a Section 368 merger. Most importantly, this means that the target company is acquired for shares in the acquiring company.

4. The transaction must meet the "continuity of interest" and "continuity of business" tests. These tests essentially provide that the seller's company must continue in operation as part of the acquiring company for at least two years and that any shareholders in the companies being merged must retain at least a 50% ownership interest for at least two years. The 50% is measured as a percentage of the ownership interest sold to the acquirer (i.e., a target company's owner selling all of his or her stock would have to retain shares in the new company equal to 50% of what he or she sold for two years). However, under a January 28, 1998, IRS ruling, this test would be met if, before that time, shares acquired in the transaction are sold to an "unrelated third party." As detailed below, an ESOP might meet this test, but there has been no confirmation of this and some experts are skeptical.

Three approaches seem practical to meet these criteria:

Straight Acquisition

In this approach, the acquirer merges with the target, with the owner of the target taking shares in the acquirer as consideration for the value of his or her ownership. These shares can then be sold to the acquirer's ESOP, and the seller can take Section 1042 treatment. The key element of this approach is that the ESOP be considered an "unrelated third party." In other aspects of tax taw, an ESOP is considered an unrelated third party. For instance, if Section 1042 is not elected in an ESOP sale, the seller still qualifies for capital gains treatment because the ESOP is considered an unrelated third party (required for such treatment). The IRS ruling on this issue, however, does not specifically say that sales to an ESOP in the scenario described here would qualify, and there have been informal indications that the IRS may not sustain this interpretation.

Reverse Merger

A common alternative is a reverse merger. In this approach, the acquiring company is merged into the target company first. The new company would meet the "continuity of business" test, assuming its business was still operated by the acquiring firm. Because the test would apply now only to the shareholders of the acquiring firm (their shares are being exchanged for the target's), as long as they do not sell 50% or more of the stock in two years, the continuity of interest test is also met. Meanwhile, the new company could immediately reassume the name of the firm that wants to do the acquisition. The owner of the target can now sell to the ESOP and take advantage of Section 1042, assuming the 30% ESOP ownership of total shares in the merged company is met.

The "Two-ESOP" Approach

This appears to be the most common model now. It involves both the target and acquiring company setting up ESOPs. Typically, the acquirer will have had an ESOP in place well before the transaction. The target company's owner sells to the newly established target ESOP in a transaction that may be financed by the acquirer and takes Section 1042 treatment. Immediately thereafter, the acquiring company's ESOP merges with the target's ESOP. Typically, the acquiring company's ESOP would now own a majority of the target's shares (because the ESOP in the target had at least a majority). Target company ESOP participants can now participate in the ESOP of the acquiring company (technically, because target is a member of acquirer's control group).

At least one or two years later, the two companies actually merge. The delay is necessary to meet tax rules concerning tax-free reorganizations, although there may be specific exemptions for unusual circumstances. This approach has been used in at least one transaction that received a private letter ruling from the IRS.

Using an ESOP to Buy Out a Division of Another Company

This application is a variation on the capital acquisition theme. When parent companies are looking to divest divisions or subsidiaries, they often will want to find a synergistic buyer who can offer a premium price. In other cases, however, there either is no such buyer or the company offers to sell to employees, perhaps out of a sense of obligation, to bolster employee morale at other operations, or because of outside pressure.

In these cases, the employees usually form an acquisition company. The company borrows enough money to purchase the assets of the division or subsidiary. At the same time, the new company sets up an ESOP. The company reloans the money it has borrowed to the ESOP, which the ESOP uses to buy shares in the company. The company now takes the loan proceeds and uses them to buy the assets. Alternatively, the ESOP could buy the assets and exchange them for stock. Either way, as the loan is repaid to the ESOP, shares are released to employee accounts.

Structuring the ESOP is the easy part. The real questions in these transactions are feasibility and finance. For the transaction to be feasible, all the usual elements of a sensible business plan must be in place—money, markets, and management. In many spin-off situations, the division or subsidiary may not have developed a management group capable of taking both entrepreneurial and administrative leadership. The new company will also be burdened with a lot of non-productive debt that must be paid fairly quickly. Buyouts are also often hampered by the parent company's desire to compete in similar markets. The sale may be occurring in the first place because the parent does not think much of the markets the division or subsidiary serves. The best candidates, therefore, tend to be operations with solid markets or management whose line of business are no longer of interest to the parent but whose business prospects are not so stellar as to attract other buyers. Often, there is an identifiable missing piece in these operations, such as bad employee morale, excessive overhead charges by the parent, a lack of parent interest in potentially successful ideas or initiatives from the division or subsidiary, or high labor costs that could be reduced by an ESOP in which employees take concessions. Operations that are simply losing money in depressed markets despite the parent's best efforts are almost never good candidates, while star operations can almost never be bought by employees because someone else will pay more.

The second major hurdle is finance. In most of these buyouts, equity capital is essential. Lenders are not going to lend 100% of the value of a company except in the most unusual circumstances. This equity can take many forms, and often combines a number of elements. Where a great deal of capital is needed, there are specialized investment firms that will purchase a large, usually majority, stake in these companies with the intention of selling to the ESOP over time. Management will almost always be asked to invest its own cash, as much to provide some "skin in the game" to encourage them to stay as to generate capital. High-risk lenders may provide subordinated debt, usually at very high prices. Some states will provide loans or loan guarantees. Parent companies might retain partial ownership or invest in the transaction. Finally, employees will often be asked to contribute, sometimes directly through the purchase of shares and (more often) through wage and benefit concessions.

Buyouts of this kind are expensive to organize, time-consuming, and riskier than other ESOP transactions. They also raise more complicated issues, such as allocating equity between direct investors who risk their own cash and the ESOP, which borrows money on a non-recourse basis on behalf of employees. Few investors will be willing to take a dollar in equity for a dollar in cash if the ESOP gets a dollar in equity for a dollar in borrowed money to be repaid by the company. There are ways to structure these transactions to accommodate everyone's interests, but they take a high level of expertise and can be controversial between the parties involved.

Despite all these issues, when a division or subsidiary is for sale and employees are logical buyers, an ESOP can be a very desirable solution, giving employees a chance to become owners and, in some cases, saving their jobs as well.

Using an ESOP to Save a Failing Company

One of the most publicized, but least common, applications of an ESOP is to save a failing company. Often this will be a division or subsidiary of another company, and will follow the scenario above, usually with a strong emphasis on substantial concessions, often in the 10% to 30% range. In other cases, it will be to buy a stand-alone company. The mechanisms for this kind of sale would be similar, but the management problem is usually more acute. Clearly, old management will need to be replaced, so the first issue will be to find out if there is competent new management willing to enter the picture in what will be a very uncertain new company.

Another scenario is the one followed at a number of airline, steel, and trucking companies in the 1980s and a handful of other companies in the 1990s. Here the employees, often represented by a union, agree to take concessions in return for stock. This was the basic structure of the United Airlines transaction, although United was not in danger of failing (instead, employees saw the danger of the company breaking into four different companies, some of which would pay lower wages). In most of these cases, the plan is time-limited; the ESOP will last only as long as the concessions. During that time, employees typically are given some governance rights, commonly minority representation on the board.

The total buyouts have had a reasonably good track record, given their often dire circumstances; a study by the NCEO in the 1980s found that 60% lasted over five years, and another 20% were sold to other companies. Just 20% closed. Buyouts became much less common in the 1990s, but anecdotally, most seem to still be in business, and some are doing very well. Wage-for-stock deals have fared less well. Most of the companies involved closed within a few years. The ones that survived rarely continued their ESOPs, or like United, froze them so that new employees were not included. More importantly, employers and employees in these companies viewed the plans as temporary and there were few, if any, efforts to create the kind of ownership culture that can help turn companies around. By contrast, most of the outright buyouts did make such efforts.

Using an ESOP to Bolster the Market for Thinly Traded Shares

Finally, ESOPs can be used to help support trading in thinly traded stocks. By far the most common use of this application is in community banks. These institutions, as well as some other businesses, often have a large number of individual or institutional owners, most of whom own a relatively small percentage of the company. Providing a market for their shares can be difficult. The company can buy back the shares, but it is an after-tax expense. Other owners may want to buy, but only on an occasional basis that will have difficulty matching buyers and sellers. If the stock is traded on the "pink sheets" or a regional stock market, there may not be enough activity to support more than periodic trades. This lack of liquidity will lower the share price to an amount closer to what the price would be if the company were closely held.

An ESOP can, within limits, help solve this problem. The ESOP can use cash reserves from company contributions (remember, companies can contribute cash as well as stock to an ESOP as long as the ESOP remains primarily invested in company stock) or can borrow money to buy stock from owners wanting to sell. This creates liquidity in private companies and strengthens the market in thinly traded public companies. The ESOP cannot be compelled to buy shares, however. The ESOP must determine that the price is fair and that timing of the purchase is appropriate for the best interests of plan participants.

Conclusion

ESOPs are an exceptional vehicle for providing for business continuity, but, as this chapter shows, they have many other applications. It is critical to remember, however, that whatever financial objectives an ESOP is being used to accomplish, it is first and foremost an employee benefit plan. The decision to implement an ESOP, and the way it is subsequently run, must be made with an eye first toward whether the plan is good for employees. As research described elsewhere in this book has shown, plans that are run this way help companies make more money. This added productivity is, in the end, the best reason to use an ESOP.

CHAPTER 12

ESOPs and Corporate Performance

Corey Rosen

The research on employee ownership and corporate performance comes to a very definite conclusion: the combination of ownership and participative management is a powerful competitive tool. Neither ownership nor participation alone, however, accomplishes very much. The findings also seem to apply primarily to closely held companies. Research indicates that public companies generally do not view employee ownership as much more than another corporate benefit. For this and other reasons explored below, the relationship between employee ownership and corporate performance in public companies is ambiguous.

The 2000 Rutgers Study

In 2000, in the largest and most significant study to date on the performance of ESOPs in closely held companies, Douglas Kruse and Joseph Blasi, both of Rutgers University, found that ESOPs increase sales, employment, and sales per employee by about 2.3% to 2.4% per year over what would have been expected absent an ESOP. ESOP companies are also somewhat more likely to still be in business several years later. This is despite (or perhaps because of) the fact that ESOP companies are substantially more likely than comparable companies to offer other retirement benefit plans along with their ESOP.

Kruse and Blasi obtained files from Dun & Bradstreet on ESOP companies that had adopted plans between 1988 and 1994. They then matched these companies to non-ESOP companies that were comparable in size, industry, and region. They then looked for which of these com-

panies had sales and employment data available for a period three years
before the plan's start and three years after. The sales and employment
growth data were then compared for each year for each paired company.
They also checked the companies' filings with the Department of Labor
to determine which of the companies had other retirement-oriented benefit plans. Finally, they looked to see what percentage of the companies
remained in business in the 1995 through 1997 period.

The process yielded 343 ESOP companies and 343 matched pairs
for the overall sample. However, missing information meant that employment data were available only for 254 ESOP companies and 234
matched pairs: 138 ESOP companies and 77 matched pairs for sales, and
115 ESOP companies and 65 pairs for sales per employee (some matched
companies could be used for more than one ESOP company).

The results showed that ESOP companies performed better in the
post-ESOP period than their pre-ESOP performance would have pre-
dicted: Annual sales growth increased by 2.4%, annual employment
growth increased by 2.3%, and annual growth in sales per employee
increased by 2.3% in the post-ESOP period relative to what would have
been expected based on growth during the pre-ESOP period.

It might be assumed that sales per employee would not go up by
2.3% per year since sales and employment growth differences were about
the same, but, the researchers explain, the differing compositions of the
samples for the measures makes such a simple comparison misleading.
The relative growth numbers might seem small at first glance, but projected out over 10 years, an ESOP company with these differentials would
be a third larger than its paired non-ESOP match.

The 1987 NCEO Study

The first study to show a specific causal linkage between employee ownership and corporate performance was by Michael Quarrey and Corey
Rosen of the NCEO. The study looked at the performance of employee
ownership companies for five years before and after they set up their
employee stock ownership plans (ESOPs). The study adjusted for market and industry fluctuations by comparing ESOP company performance
relative to competitor performance both before and after adoption of the
ESOP. Thus, only improvements in the ESOP company's performance

relative to competitors after ESOP adoption would be measured as a positive impact on performance. For example, if a company were growing 3% per year faster than its competitors in the pre-ESOP period, and 6% per year faster in the post-ESOP period, there would be a 3% gain attributable to the ESOP, other things being equal.

The study found that ESOP companies had sales growth rates 3.4% per year higher and employment growth rates 3.8% per year higher in the post-ESOP period than would have been expected based on pre-ESOP performance. When the companies were divided into three groups based on how participatively managed they were, however, only the most participative companies showed a gain. These companies grew 8% to 11% per year faster than they would have been expected to grow without an ESOP, while the middle group showed little change, and the bottom group showed a decline in performance.

Participation alone has not been shown to improve performance. A large number of studies show that the impact of participation absent ownership is short-lived or ambiguous. Ownership seems to provide the cultural glue to keep participation going.

The New York and Washington State Studies

In 1992, economist Gorm Winther and colleagues in New York and Washington State followed up the NCEO study, using the same research design but different samples: 1 of 25 employee ownership firms in New York State and 1 of 28 employee ownership companies in Washington State. In both studies, employee ownership alone had little or no impact on corporate performance, but a substantial impact when combined with participative management. In Washington, companies that combined ownership and participation grew in employment 10.9% per year more than would have been expected. Sales grew 6% per year more. The New York results used correlations and cannot be compared directly, but the results were in the same direction. In Washington, majority employee-owned firms that were participatively managed did even better.

The Washington study also found that the synergistic effect of actual ownership and participation was more powerful than that between profit sharing and participation; the positive results held true even when the control group companies had no employee ownership but did have profit sharing and participation programs.

The GAO Study

In 1987, the U.S. General Accounting Office (GAO) conducted a before-and-after study using methodology similar to the NCEO study, but focusing on productivity and profitability with a sample of 110 firms. The GAO found little correlation between performance and ownership except when looking at ESOP firms with high levels of employee participation. Participatively managed employee ownership firms increased their productivity growth rate by 52% per year. For example, if a company's productivity growth rate were 3.0% per year before adopting an ESOP, it would be 4.5% afterwards.

The lack of significant findings in other areas could be counter-indicative to the other studies reported here. However, the methods the GAO used were controversial and likely resulted in conservative productivity measures. Because it assumed that employee ownership companies did not increase overall compensation when they set up an ESOP, while evidence, as sited in the next study, indicates that they do, the GAO study probably underestimated the positive impact of employee ownership on productivity.

The Impact of ESOPs on Employee Compensation

Providing strong backing to the argument that ESOPs do increase compensation for employees—and therefore that the GAO study underestimates the positive impact they have on performance—is a 1998 study by Peter Kardas and Jim Keogh of the Washington Department of Community, Trade, and Economic Development, and Adria Scharf of the University of Washington. Their research shows that, in fact, employees are significantly better compensated in ESOP companies than are employees in comparable non-ESOP companies. Using 1995 employment and wage data from the Washington State Employment Security Department, and 1995 data on retirement benefits from a survey of companies and from federal Form 5500, the study matched up 102 ESOP companies with

499 comparison companies matched in terms of industrial classification and employment size. The median hourly wage in the ESOP firms was 5% to 12% higher than the median hourly wage in the comparison companies, depending on the wage level.

The study found the average value of all retirement benefits in ESOP companies was equal to $32,213, with an average value in the comparison companies of about $12,735. Looking only at retirement plan assets other than ESOPs, the ESOP companies had an average value of $7,952, compared to $12,735 for non-ESOP companies. Given that the typical ESOP is actually about 20% invested in diversified assets other than company stock, employees in ESOP companies would have had about as much in diversified assets as employees would have in all assets in non-ESOP companies. In ESOP companies, the average corporate contribution per employee per year was between 9.6% and 10.8% of pay per year, depending on how it was measured. In non-ESOP companies, it was between 2.8% and 3.0%. All this clearly shows that for the majority of employees in ESOP companies, ESOP derived benefits are in addition to regular compensation—which itself is slightly higher than that for employees in non-ESOP companies.

Public Companies and Employee Ownership

The performance data for ESOPs in public companies are much more ambiguous. A 1999 study by Hamid Mehran of Northwestern University for Hewitt Associates found that ESOPs in 382 publicly traded companies increased the return on assets (ROA) 2.7% over what would otherwise have been expected. The study looked at the companies' financial returns for two years before the plan's implementation and four years after. Each company was compared to industry norm ROA figures for both periods. Mehran also found that for the 303 ESOP companies surviving the entire four year post-ESOP study period, ROA was 14% higher than the comparison group scores, while for the 382 companies as a group, ROA was 6.9% higher.

Over 60% of the companies experienced an increase in stock price in the two-day period following the public announcement of the ESOP, with the average increase for all companies at 1.6%. This suggests that the stock market now reacts positively to ESOPs, a change from the pattern in the 1980s when ESOP announcements were often seen as an indicator that a company was trying to prevent a hostile takeover.

In 1992, Douglas Kruse and Joseph Blasi of Rutgers University and Michael Conte of the University of Baltimore created an "Employee Ownership Index" (EOI). The EOI tracks the average percentage increase in stock price of all publicly traded companies with a public record of 10% or more employee ownership and more than $50 million in market value. The EOI grew 193% from 1992 through 1997, while the Dow was up 145% and the S&P 500 increased 140%. The authors do not attribute any causal relationship to these numbers, however.

Other studies look at before-and-after results, with mixed conclusions. Donald Collat, in a 1995 study, found that public companies that did not set up their ESOPs in response to a takeover threat saw their operating margins improve 2.1% per year compared to their pre-ESOP performance. The study looked at companies for three years before and after the ESOP, indexing for market effects. Takeover-threat ESOPs, however, saw a decline of 3.3%. In a 1996 study, Mary Ducy, Zahid Igbal, and Aige Akhigbe found that ESOP companies showed a decline in operating cash flow of 0.2% to 2.1% post-ESOP, also using a three years before/three years after measure, and again indexing for market effects. While these are the most thorough of several studies on public company ESOPs, other studies come to a similarly mixed conclusion.

Finally, a 1998 study by Margaret Blair, Douglas Kruse, and Joseph Blasi found that companies that are publicly traded and at least 20% or more owned by an ESOP are more organizationally stable than comparable non-ESOP companies. Looking at data between 1983 and 1996, the study found that 74.1% of the ESOP companies remained as independent operations while only 37.8% of the comparison companies did so. These figures changed to 59.3% and 51.1% respectively for the period 1983 through 1997. None of the ESOP companies went bankrupt, but 25% of the comparison companies did.

These mixed results are probably explained by three factors. First, a 1997 NCEO study found that public companies generally seem to view employee ownership solely as a benefit plan, not part of an explicit organizational culture, as many closely held companies do. Second, ESOPs in public companies tend to own a much smaller percentage of company stock than ESOPs in closely held companies. Some studies have indicated this is a factor in how effective ESOPs are. Finally, in many cases, public company ESOPs simply replaced existing plans, such as 401(k) plans, through which the company contributed company stock to employees. Hence, the "before" was really not much different from the "after," so not much could be expected to change.

Other Studies

Several other studies suggest positive relationships but were not able to show causality. A 1990 study by the Michigan Center for Employee Ownership and Gainsharing and Michigan State University asked executives to indicate whether employee ownership (about 90% of the employee ownership plans were ESOPs) had an impact on sales, profits, productivity and other measures. The results were very positive. They were the most positive, in keeping with the trends in other studies, in companies that scored high on participative management measures. Majority employee-owned companies also did better than minority employee-owned companies. In addition, the study found that the incidence of employee participation programs, such as work teams and advisory councils, increased 50% to 100% after an employee ownership plan was set up.

A 1993 Northeast Ohio Employee Ownership Center study also found dramatic increases in participation after an ESOP was set up, with the incidence of programs such as team-based management and participation training programs doubling in most cases. The study did not provide before-and-after data, but it did find that employee-owned companies outperformed competitors on job-growth measures 49% of the time, performed similarly 50% of the time, and performed worse only 1% of the time.

Conclusion

Researchers now agree that "the case is closed" on employee ownership and corporate performance. Findings this consistent are very unusual. We can say with certainty that when ownership and participative management are combined, substantial gains result. Ownership alone and participation alone, however, have, at best, spotty or short-lived results.

CHAPTER 13

ESOPs and Corporate Governance

Edward J. Carberry

One of the issues that most concern business owners when setting up an ESOP is whether employees will have a role in corporate governance. While some owners are concerned to find effective ways to get people involved at the highest levels of the company, most are worried that employee owners will have too much power. In fact, the large majority of ESOP companies end up being governed much as they were prior to the ESOP. The existing board and management usually remain intact except for normal turnover. ESOP rules require only the most nominal employee control rights. When companies voluntarily go beyond this, the results have normally been positive. A National Center for Employee Ownership study found that employees tend to be conservative shareholders and that directors and managers of these companies make decisions similar to those made by investor and management-controlled firms.

The only governance mechanism for employee owners that the law addresses in a detailed way is voting rights. This does not mean that employee owners have substantial power through the voting process, although in certain situations, they can have considerable impact. Their power as shareholders is limited by both the laws that govern employee ownership plans as well as the obstacles faced by shareholders in general. Their actual power depends on plan rules, whether or not the company is private or public, the percentage of stock owned by the plan, as well as the level of communication and awareness among employee owners.

The median level of ownership by an ESOP in private companies is 30% to 40%, and many are majority owned. In public companies, the median ownership level is about 10%, and only a handful of the 1,000 or so public company ESOPs own a majority of the stock.

ESOP shares are held in a trust fund and are therefore legally owned by the plan's trustee until employees leave the company. The ESOP trustee is generally the fiduciary responsible for overseeing the plan's operation and is appointed by the company. A fiduciary is defined as the person who makes decisions for the plan, whatever that person's formal responsibility is (if someone tells a trustee how to vote, that person, not the trustee, is the fiduciary). Although trustees can be anyone (an employee, manager, director, or outside party), they are usually a member of management. Some larger companies appoint an independent trustee, such as one from a bank trust department. In most companies, either an ESOP committee or someone in management directs the trustee. An ESOP committee can be appointed by management, elected by employees, or a combination of both.

The trustee's duties include ensuring that the plan complies with all applicable laws and that it operates according to the specific plan document. The trustee is in charge of administering the plan; communicating with employees how the plan operates and issuing an annual statement; making decisions relating to how the shares are valued, how they are distributed, and whether or not they are bought or sold. Trustees have a legal obligation (also known as a "fiduciary" responsibility) to act prudently and in the exclusive interest of plan participants.

The trustee also votes the ESOP shares and can be independent or directed (meaning someone else, usually management, tells them how to vote or tender shares). Participants, however, are required to direct the trustee on how to vote the shares in their accounts on certain issues. The type and variety of these issues depends on whether or not the company is privately or publicly held.

In *privately held companies,* ESOP participants must be able to direct the trustee on how to the vote the shares in their accounts in a limited number of situations, including those related to merger, consolidation, recapitalization, reclassification, liquidation, dissolution or a substantial sale of the company's assets. Employee participants do not have to be able to direct the trustee as to the voting of shares for board members nor the sale or merger of the company in a stock transaction. Participants vote the shares in their accounts regardless of how much they are vested, and voting can be done on either a one share/one vote basis or a one-person/one vote basis, if the company chooses to write the plan this way. Privately held companies can, if they wish, pass through full voting rights to ESOP participants. At least 20% (and as many as 40% by some estimates) of private company ESOPs do this.

Also, in a leveraged ESOP that has obtained financing from a lender receiving tax benefits from Section 133 of the IRS Code (which allowed the lender to exclude 50% of the interest received on an ESOP loan), full voting rights must be passed through to the shares of ESOP participants that have been acquired through the loan. Section 133 was repealed in 1996, so this only applies to those companies still under its strictures.

In *publicly traded ESOP companies*, ESOP participants must be able to direct the trustee on how to vote the shares in their accounts on all shareholder issues. This typically includes electing the boards of directors, voting on major corporate decisions, and voting on shareholder resolutions that have been submitted. This does not necessarily include the right to direct the trustee as to the tendering of shares, although the company can pass through this right. In fact, most public companies with ESOPs do pass through this right in order to place stock into friendly hands in the event of a hostile takeover. Voting must be done on a one share/one vote basis. Many public companies with leveraged ESOPs also provide mirror voting and tendering rules for unallocated shares, meaning trustees vote or tender these shares in the same proportion as allocated shares.

The Role of the ESOP Trustee in Voting the Shares

Employee owners in an ESOP company do not usually possess a great deal of direct voting power. For most decisions in privately held companies, the ESOP trustee votes the shares held by the ESOP. Normally, the trustee has the "fiduciary" role of being responsible for decisions, but this can be assigned to someone else. Although trustees in public companies must accept direction from ESOP participants on more decisions, this often does not translate into a great deal of power.

The trustee's behavior is primarily regulated by the Employee Retirement Income Security Act (ERISA), which requires that trustees act prudently and for the exclusive benefit of plan participants. In terms of corporate governance, ERISA is narrow in scope. Its primary purpose is to protect the retirement benefits of employees. The predominant role it gives to the trustee is to maximize the value of employee holdings; it does not address the issues of giving employees a greater role in governance. Trustees are, for the most part, limited to considering financial issues when voting the stock or making other decisions. ERISA does not, for example, require that ESOPs pass through the full incidental rights of ownership to ESOP participants, including the right to obtain detailed information on the corporation, the ability to nominate directors, the ability to initiate a shareholder's resolution, and the right to tender shares.

While "acting in the best interests of plan participants" connotes that decisions are clear-cut, the issues can, and have, become complicated. For example, are the interests of plan participants defined in the short or long term? If the trustee is a member of management or directed by management (and it usually is), how can he or she remain partial to employee interests when these interests conflict with those of management? Trustees may, in practice, consider non-economic issues, such as long-term employment, but ERISA seems to clearly exclude them. Are their ways to write plans so that these types of issues can be considered? Also, how can trustees legally protect themselves if they are voting according to the directions of plan participants when these directions do not seem to be in the participants' best interests? Should trustees always conduct their own investigation of the issues, even when they are directed? While a set of concrete standards has not emerged from the case law, and trustees can never be absolutely sure about what to do in every situation, some common themes have been expressed and can serve as general guidelines for trustee behavior.

When trustees vote the shares, they must make an independent investigation of the issues and vote for the exclusive benefit of plan participants. This is *the* general guideline that should govern a trustee's behavior in any decision. Trustees must obtain as much relevant information as needed and judge it exclusively with the goal of maximizing the assets held by the plan. When deciding on a purchase or sale of stock, for example, trustees must try to get the best price possible and obtain all the necessary financial information to make that decision. Whether *directed* trustees must follow this standard is controversial; limited case law suggests they can pass on fiduciary obligations to whomever directs them, provided they do not violate the plan or ERISA. This is an ambiguous standard, however, that has not been clearly defined.

When participants direct the trustee, trustees must ensure that plan participants have access to adequate, unbiased information and override their vote only if there is compelling evidence that their decision is not in their long-term interest. Generally, if a plan document allows plan participants to direct the trustee on how to vote on certain issues or whether to tender shares, the trustee has a legal obligation to accept these directions and follow the plan document as closely as possible. This does not necessarily mean, however, that trustees should blindly accept the directions of plan participants. Trustees can override these directions if they feel that they are not in the best interest of plan participants or if they feel participants were coerced or misinformed, but they must have significant evidence to act in this way. It is easier for trustees to justify ignoring participant directions in decisions where there is a direct financial judgment involved.

As noted above, when other parties provide direction on voting decisions, the liability of trustees can be diminished. These other parties can be considered "named fiduciaries" and can include anyone who contributes to making voting decisions or others relating to the operation of the plan: plan participants, an administrative committee, management, etc. Trustees are not absolved of all responsibility, but their role as the primary fiduciary can be mitigated in these situations.

When trustees are required to make an independent decision, and it appears that they have a conflict of interest, they should appoint an independent trustee who can act in this capacity. It is essential for trustees to remain neutral and comply with all applicable corporate and securities laws when a company is involved in a proxy fight. Especially when ESOP shares are the swing vote in a battle for control, ESOP trustees should consider hiring an outside trustee. If plan documents are drafted so that employees can direct the voting or tendering of the shares, then they must be given unbiased information, preferably prepared by an outsider, and should be named as fiduciaries for their own accounts.

Practical Issues in Closely Held Companies

Most companies considering an ESOP are closely held. Most will not want to change their governance structure, at least not at first. For them, the practical issues are simple: design the plan so that the board of directors appoints or controls the trustee. The trustee then elects the board. The trustee still must adhere to fiduciary duties, but conflicts between these interests and the interests of the board are not common. Explaining to employees why they do not have control rights is trickier, however. Many employees expect that ownership implies voting. They may see the ESOP as a sham if they do not have this right. Companies need to explain that ESOP ownership is different from other ownership in that employees do not actually purchase the shares, nor are they personally responsible for corporate debts the way some owners may be. As people take different risks with ownership, they get different ownership rights.

Some companies are reluctant to discuss this "downside" of ownership with employees, but failing to do so is a major error. Being up-front and straightforward about the rights and responsibilities of ownership is essential to making employees feel like they are being treated as responsible adults.

A significant minority of companies, however, want employees to participate at the management level. There are a number of ways to do this. Employees can elect some or all board members. A certain number of board seats can be set aside for employees to be appointed by management or an employee committee. Alternatively, employees might elect several people as possible candidates, and the board could choose among them. However employees join the board, they should be provided with the requisite financial and legal education to understand their responsibilities. Feedback mechanisms between the employee board members and employees would be set up to take advantage of the communications opportunities this provides between management and the work force.

If board membership is not desired, a company can set up an employee advisory committee to meet with the board, but that will not have formal corporate fiduciary responsibilities. This group, which is usually elected, serves as a good way to express employees concerns to management or vice-versa.

Apart from this, employees can participate on an ESOP committee that directs the plan's fiduciary. Here too, employees can be either elected or appointed as a majority or minority of the committee, and here too they should receive appropriate training.

Conclusion

Corporate governance in ESOPs is not what it may seem at first blush. It is clearly not as threatening to existing management as it might seem, both because the laws require such minimal participation and because employees tend to act conservatively even when given broader rights than are required. On the other hand, fiduciary duties imposed on the trustee require a high level of diligence and integrity, and communicating ownership rights to employees must be done in a careful and open manner. Where employees take a larger governance role, they need appropriate education to act responsibly. If these requirements are met, corporate governance issues should proceed smoothly, whether employees have few rights or many.

CHAPTER 14

An Introduction to Ownership Management

Corey Rosen

Imagine you were given two choices about your dinner tonight. For the first choice, you would be taken to a nice place, where you could help select what you wanted to eat, soak up the ambiance, smell the aromas, and even help pay for the meal. But you couldn't eat it because all you were going to get was a "sense of dinner."

Alternatively, imagine you could go to the same restaurant. This time, food would be ordered for you, based on what someone else thought you should eat. You would have to finish in a set time, eating food in the order and with the amount of salt and pepper recommended. And you would still help pay for it.

Neither choice is very satisfying, of course. Imagine now that you work for a company. Ms. Bigg, the vice-president, tells the employees that, starting this year, the company wants everyone to have a "sense of ownership." The employees would be expected now to make more decisions, take more responsibility, and know more about the company's finances. In other words, they would be asked to think and act like owners—but they would not actually get any ownership.

Meanwhile, at another company, employees are given ownership as a result of an ESOP set up to buy out a departing owner. The plan was introduced with great fanfare. In this company too management hoped the employees would "think and act like owners." The truth is, however, that employees actually have little opportunity to do so because management is reluctant to share financial information, to listen to employee ideas, or to give employees greater responsibility for making decisions.

Like our imaginary dinners, neither company is as satisfying to employees as it could be. "A sense of ownership" is not real ownership. And the financial rewards of equity without the opportunity to be more involved in what is now your company can be very frustrating. If you have ideas and information you believe can improve company performance but no one will listen, being told you are an owner can be more grating than motivating.

A company can provide more than a sense of ownership by putting all the attributes of ownership together. Such companies share real equity ownership, teach employees to understand company finances, and provide regular and meaningful opportunities for employees to have input into how their jobs are performed. In the words of business writer John Case, they seek to create a "company of business people." The research on these companies decisively shows that they perform substantially better than they would under a more traditional management approach. At the same time, they create workplaces that provide people with a level of dignity and reward rarely found in other companies.

Ownership and Participation

It may seem obvious that if employees are owners, they will work harder, and if they work harder the company will perform better. What seems obvious is not always true, however. To find out more about the impact of ownership, researchers have conducted several major studies.

We at the National Center for Employee Ownership (NCEO) published the first major study on this topic in the September/October 1987 issue of the *Harvard Business Review*. In general, we found that over a 10-year period, ESOP companies grew 40% to 46% faster with their employee ownership plan than they would have without it. The results were carefully controlled to eliminate any other factors, such as changes in the overall performance of the industry, changes in management, or a general pattern of better growth within the company.

That was good news for employee ownership. But on closer examination, we found that most of this growth was accounted for by a minority of companies with highly participative management styles. These companies grew 11% to 17% per year faster than the least participative companies, and the least participative companies actually performed worse after their employee ownership plans were established. Does that mean that it was really participation, not ownership, that made the difference? Not really. A large number of studies on this issue show that participation, on its own, has only a small positive impact on corporate performance. The combination of ownership and participation, on the other hand, yields impressive results.

In the years after we completed our study, other studies by the U.S. General Accounting Office (GAO) and by university researchers in New York, Indiana, and Washington came to precisely the same conclusion: ownership on its own has, at best, a small positive impact, but ownership and participation combined have a very dramatic effect. The Washington researchers also found that profit sharing and participation do not have the same combined explanatory effect that ownership and participation do. This study and others are summarized elsewhere in this book in the chapter on corporate performance.

Why Participation Matters

Why doesn't ownership itself matter more? The findings may be easier to understand in the context of what actually happens in a company every day. An employee owner comes to work with a clear financial stake in the company. For some employees, this will increase their commitment. To some extent, just working harder, or more carefully, will make a difference in itself. There will be less waste, customers will be greeted more cheerfully, there will be less turnover, and there may be more actual work done per hour. In most companies, however, all of these things will make only incremental differences to the bottom line. Labor costs are only part of total costs (10% to 50% in most companies), only some workers will actually change their behavior (typically about half, partly because some people are already working as hard as they can), and the total amount of additional "incentive-driven" work that can realistically be expected is relatively small (30 minutes more a day is just 6.7% of total labor costs). In fact, we at the NCEO have done calculations of how much "working harder" alone might save in a number of companies and typically find the bottom-line impact is only about a 1% increase.

At this point, you might be thinking, "Yes, but the real issue is to get people to work smarter." We'd take it one step further: the real issue is to get whole organizations to work smarter. Organizations work smarter when they use information better. Their people have ideas about how to make their product or service better, or less expensive, or both. They create more new products and new markets. They create new ways to organize the flow of work so that fewer people can do more things with the same or less effort. To make a smarter organization, a company needs as many of its people as possible engaged in the task of thinking about how everything the company does can be done better.

In conventional companies, it is up to managers both to generate the information needed to make changes and to come up with the ideas for making improvements. Information moves up and down several layers of the organization, slowing the process of decision-making considerably.

Until recently, this conventional system of management worked acceptably. Before the advent of the computer, products and markets changed slowly. Companies had the time to develop standardized procedures and keep them in place for years. Information processing and analysis was a slow, complicated job that required special skills. It made sense to organize a company so that these analytical skills were segregated among those able to do the task, while employees were trained to carry out standard procedures developed by others.

That luxury no longer exists. Product life cycles are vastly shorter. Markets are increasingly segmented and specialized and change very quickly. Information can be received, processed, and analyzed by computers in seconds. The sheer volume of information now available is orders of magnitude larger. All this information is also now available in usable formats to many more people than before. The machine operator now knows a lot more about how that machine works than a manager did a decade ago; the customer service representative looking at a screen of information knows more about the customers than managers ever knew just a few years ago. Companies can ignore these changes and plod along, restricting decisions and information to a select group, waiting for management meetings and executive approval to make changes. But they cannot succeed this way. The winners of the next decade will be companies that have more people processing more information and making more decisions faster. These will be the companies that stay ahead of the market or even learn to shape it.

Employees are the best and most abundant source of information. They are often the ones dealing directly with customers, suppliers, machines, technologies, and each other. They have ideas and experiences that can contribute to making the company work better. But in most companies, they are given neither the incentive nor the opportunity to share their knowledge, and managers have neither the training nor the motivation to listen to them even if they do. Employee owners have the motivation, but unless there are regular, clear opportunities to share their knowledge, it is unlikely they will do so.

What does it take to enable an employee to tell another employee or a manager that something should be changed, or that there is something they should know? First, there has to be an opportunity. Do employees even have a time and place to talk to other people? Second, there has to be an expectation that the employee is responsible for sharing ideas and information. Most employees are reluctant to speak up, or even to think in terms of making suggestions, and need a lot of encouragement. Third, management must be willing to listen. Sometimes managers behave as if they are interested, but do not act on an employee's idea because they feel that would undermine their own position. Fourth, employees need to know that their ideas actually get used, or be told why doing so is not practical.

Just having employees share ideas and information, however, is not enough. Giving people a clear financial understanding of the company will make these efforts even more productive. That is why almost all employee ownership companies now share financial information with employees, and many practice "open-book management" or the "Great Game of Business" (an approach developed by employee-owned Springfield ReManufacturing Corporation, now called SRC Holdings). These techniques involve training employees to read detailed financial and performance data and apply this context to the decisions they make every day. Open-book management practices are one of the fastest growing trends not just in employee ownership firms, but in business generally. As SRC Holdings' CEO Jack Stack puts it, asking people to play the business game without telling them the financials is like asking people to play a game of basketball but not letting them know the score.

Most of the companies that succeed with participation either explicitly or implicitly have a central organizing theme, such as employee participation groups, teams, committees, task forces, cells, electronic systems, training, or financials. These themes help keep people focused and give the process more direction. They are not so pervasive, however, that they restrict companies from implementing participation outside the core concept.

It is important to remember that participation is a process, not a program. While every company has a number of specific things it does, the key to success is not so much the structures used, but the commitment to finding ways to create a participation process. Different companies have developed lots of good ideas to create an environment where participation is welcomed. The specific mechanisms ultimately matter less than creating a company where employees feel not only comfortable but also compelled to see that things are done as well as possible.

What Is Participative Management?

Participative management is a term that is often used and even praised but not very well defined. To some people, it just means having an "open door." To others, it means setting up an elaborate decision-making web in a company in which everyone shares decisions about everything affecting them. It does, however, have several key components:

1. Decisions are made by people, individually or as teams, based on their knowledge and involvement in the issue at hand, not on their job titles.

2. There is a bias for getting people to share ideas and information before a decision is made. Often this will be through a meeting of those involved, but other mechanisms, such as e-mail, suggestion/feedback systems, "management by walking around," or even informal networks and conversations are important as well.

3. People are given the financial and performance data needed to make a good decision and the training needed to understand it.

4. Work processes are organized into functional teams (teams of people working in the same area), cross-functional teams (teams assembled from different areas to assess the impact of decisions in one area on another), and ad hoc teams (temporary teams formed to solve particular problems) whenever the ideas and information of more than one or two people are desirable.

5.   Individuals are given as much job responsibility as they can handle, not as little as they need to function.

The emphasis on meetings and teams grows out of the belief (confirmed by research) that groups of people usually make better decisions than individuals. Group participants can bounce ideas off each other, share information, and apply critical thinking to concepts in ways that those same people, tackling the problem alone, cannot. The group dynamic also stimulates an "aha!" effect—the phenomenon of getting an idea that would not have occurred to you otherwise because something someone says stimulates a new thought. Finally, decisions made by groups tend to be more legitimate to group members and, therefore, carried out with more enthusiasm.

While each of these principles is important, it is equally important to define which issues will not be decided in a broadly participative way. These would include those matters deemed too sensitive for group consideration (compensation and firing are two common examples), issues where expertise resides in only one or two people, where there is no time to make a group decision, or, most commonly, everyday issues where decisions are obvious or not important enough to be worth discussing. Participation takes time, and while it usually results in better decisions, better decisions are not always worth the cost of making them (a team is not needed to decide which pencils to buy) or possible to consider (if a customer needs a complaint resolved right away there shouldn't be a meeting to discuss it). Management should make it as clear as possible just which issues are open for participation and which ones are not, and why.

Formal or Informal Participation?

Participation can be both formal and informal. Informal participation includes the cooperation that often develops among co-workers. Discussions over coffee or during lunch can be important ways that people influence how things get done. Many supervisors already practice a collaborative style of management, involving many people in tackling problems. The key is developing an atmosphere of cooperation that makes people feel welcome and able to share their ideas with the most appropriate people at the appropriate time. Structures and methods are often a part of the way this comfort level is achieved, but they are only part of the participation process. People with a good idea or important information shouldn't have to wait until the next meeting to share it.

For instance, at the New York-based manufacturer, Stone Construction Equipment, the spot welders and fabricators were having difficulty in assembling a modification to one of their products. They formed a task force on their own and designed a new assembly procedure that made the job much easier and more cost-efficient. This procedure was then implemented in their other two plants.

At Fastener Industries in Cleveland, President Richard Biernacki says that when this nut and bolt manufacturer became 100% employee owned, most of the supervisors and managers knew right away that things had to be done differently. But they didn't set up a lot of programs or groups. They just started involving more people in decisions that had to be made. By doing so, they created an atmosphere that encouraged people to get involved in making things work better. For instance, when a capital expenditure is needed, the initiative comes from the shop floor. The group where the need exists then develops a proposal for it. The various departments meet as needed around specific problems.

As valuable as informal participation is, however, it is rarely enough. Employees are not accustomed to sharing their ideas and information. Neither school nor work usually prepares people to do this. When employees do have input they want to share, they are often inhibited by a lack of confidence in their way of presenting it, an ambiguity about how or with whom to share it, and an uncertainty about how it will be received. Similarly, supervisors and managers have been trained and rewarded for being able to tell people what to do and getting them to do it. Now, they are being asked to play a very different role. So for companies whose philosophy is only to encourage employees to participate informally, the results are likely to be disappointing

Formal structures help overcome this inertia by providing a specific format in which participation can occur. There are ground rules for when and how to get involved. There is a chance to observe other people participating to both learn how to do it and overcome fears of doing it at all. Successful programs of this type generate ideas within the formal structure and help overcome barriers to informal, everyday participation as well.

At United Airlines, for instance, over 100 "task teams" were formed when the company embarked on its employee ownership program. These teams consisted of people appointed by management from representative groups in the company, as well as people who volunteered to participate. The teams were charged with reviewing all aspects of the airline's operations, including developing the new United Shuttle service.

Companies do not need to be as large as United to have formal programs, however. Phelps County Bank, for instance, has 65 employees. It started its participation process with a "Problem Buster Committee" that met regularly to review suggestions, assign ad hoc teams to address problems, and present proposals to management. The system worked very well, so well that the need for the committee evaporated as employees started solving problems together at earlier stages.

Giving Employees the Tools to Participate

It is not enough just to let people make more decisions. They need to have enough information to do it well, information about their own job, the company, and the industry. Otherwise, the company runs the risk of having more people make poor decisions.

Sharing financial information is the first step in giving employees the right tools. Without this information, they are much less able to make decisions in the context of what the company really needs. One of the leading examples of sharing information is SRC Holdings (formerly known as Springfield ReManufacturing Corporation) in Springfield, Missouri. An ESOP and management bought the company from International Harvester in 1983, when it had 160 employees and a very uncertain future. Jack Stack, SRC's president, realized that for the company to survive, everyone needed to know the corporate numbers and how to affect them. So a detailed monthly income statement and balance sheet were circulated, and employees were taught to read and understand them. The numbers serve as the basis for small plant-wide meetings at which projections and variances from budget are discussed. Stack says that by providing this information, employees know the score of the "Great Game of Business," as he calls it. Just playing the game motivates people, but it also provides the kind of information they need to help them make better decisions about their own work. A shop-floor worker, for instance, can do the cost accounting on the value of buying a new machine or developing a new product. By 1998, SRC had grown to over 1,000 employees and its stock value had increased from 10 cents to over $42.

The next step is training and education. Many companies provide extensive educational opportunities for their employee owners to enable them to apply the information they receive. Quad-Graphics, a major printing company in Wisconsin, bought a nearby school to provide all employees with extensive classes on all aspects of printing.

Where Should Decisions Be Made?

Every employee cannot and should not be involved in every decision. Instead, the people most involved in an activity that will be affected, or those experiencing a problem, should be the ones involved. This may mean including people from both the specific functional area (sales representatives, for instance) as well as areas the decision would affect (the people making the product the sales representative are selling). Once the appropriate people are identified, they need to have the resources and authority to involve others when needed to generate the best possible information and ideas.

At Multi-Ad Services, printing press operators and a purchasing manager formed a cross-functional employee team to buy a new press. The approach worked so well that in 1993 it was used again to buy a $1.2 million press. Bruce Taylor, Multi-Ad's controller, points out that the people who use a machine need to be comfortable with it for it to work well anyway, so it makes sense for them to be involved in the purchasing decision.

This process often involves group decision making, but just as often it means giving individuals more authority. At Connor Formed Metal Products, a manufacturer of stampings and other metal products, a computer system has been set up so that employees have access to information previously restricted to a few managers. They can learn how the projects on which they are working are priced, what the inputs are, what the key production numbers are, etc. If they have ideas about how the project can be handled better, they can write comments on the screen, and supervisors or managers will respond. In fact, a job can be stopped by employees if they are convinced there is a better way to do it. The job cannot be restarted until the suggestion is processed. Connor's stock went up 90% in the two years after the system was started, despite an industry-wide recession.

Creating a system in which decisions are made by those with the most knowledge about the issues involved means pushing decisions down lower in the organization than most companies do. It does not mean, however, that managers and supervisors stop making decisions. There are many issues for which they have the best information or perspective to make a decision. In these cases, their authority should be paramount. For instance, imagine that an employee talked to a customer who said that a change in a product would be very attractive. The employee then meets with production people and they determine they could make the change. Finance people determine it would make a profit. But a manager may know that while it would make money, the resources devoted to that use could be better used elsewhere. Only that manager is likely to have the company-wide perspective to make that kind of decision.

Getting Started

Creating a participative culture often requires a great deal of change, and change makes people uncomfortable. Too much change at once will encounter resistance; too little, apathy. It is a difficult balance for companies to achieve, and it requires a great deal of time, energy, and perseverance.

Step 1: Reflect on Goals and Motives

First, think about why you are considering making these changes. If you view "participation" as just another technique, chances are that sooner or later, you and your co-owners will be disenchanted with the results. Employees will see these attempts to get them more "involved" as just another program that will pass. But if you view participation as a permanent commitment to create a more productive and satisfying workplace through sharing information and authority, then you and your co-owners are much more likely to succeed. Making a permanent commitment is essential if people are to make the often difficult adjustments in work styles that participation requires.

The employee response to a non-participative approach to management may be more damaging in an employee ownership company than in a traditional one because of the expectations for greater influence that often develops with ownership. When managers promote ownership to employees in order to stimulate greater motivation and productivity, they create expectations that need to be fulfilled.

On the other hand, you can take some comfort in the fact that if your motivation is based on a sincere interest in everyone benefiting through opportunities to develop new skills, apply hidden or wasted talents, and find new financial success and satisfaction in working together, then just about anything you do will help, and most people will respond with enthusiasm. As Charles Clark of Tempaco, an employee-owned distributor of heating and air conditioning controls, says, "if it is done in good faith, that comes across." Our own research has consistently found that it is the commitment of top managers to treat people as owners, and not particular structures and programs, that matters most.

Step 2: Manager Commitment

For substantial and lasting changes to occur, the company's leadership must be fully committed to creating opportunities for change. Making this commitment visible is a critical step. At Avis, Joseph Vittoria and other top managers spent months touring hundreds of Avis locations to tell people of their commitment to a new way of doing business. Karl Reuther describes his experience of introducing a participative philosophy at Reuther Mold, a company with traditions developed during 35 years of conventional managing. He had hoped that changes would come from the bottom-up, but found that people needed more direction and encouragement. He says, "I had to make dramatic changes." The new employee owners did not have much experience in the management of the firm, so Reuther also had to guide them by making suggestions. Reuther advises keeping expectations modest, because as he points out, not everyone will perceive these changes as a benevolent "gift."

Step 3: Set Up a Steering Committee

Getting other people involved in the process of planning and creating this change is the first step in demonstrating a commitment to participative management and building on the commitment of others in the organization. A steering committee that includes people from various segments and levels of the company, and if present, the union, is a good vehicle for this. These committees typically consist of five to twenty members. The committee should develop the broad outlines of how to accomplish the transition to a new operational style. Later, it can assess and redirect the program that emerges.

Step 4: Hold Small Group Meetings

You may also want to hold some small group brainstorming sessions about what a participatory company might be. One practical approach is to divide the work force into random groups of about eight people each. The groups are asked to spend 15 to 20 minutes enumerating the obstacles that prevent people from sharing ideas and information more regularly. Then they spend another five minutes reaching a consensus on the two or three most important of these. The session leader emphasizes the importance of coming up with specific ideas ("the shifts don't have a way to meet"), not general complaints ("managers don't listen"). The same process is used to come up with two or three good ways to improve sharing ideas and information. Each group designates its own leader and reporter. After the groups finish, the session leader calls on the reporters to list the results. All the results are collated together and discussed further.

Step 5: Get Information About Participation

The steering committee should familiarize itself as much as possible with the principles of participatory management. Committee members might read some articles in the business and human resource management magazines that promote this concept. The Association for Quality & Participation and the American Society for Training and Development are excellent resources. Talk with managers of other companies that are run in a participative manner. If possible, visit other employee ownership companies in your area that have a participative style.

You may need an assessment of your organization to provide a sense of the overall attitudes and expectations in the company. Spend some time in the steering committee discussing the current level of participation in your company. What opportunity do people have to influence decisions that affect them? How do different people in different parts of the organization see this? Are workers able to influence how their work is structured? Do the managers ask people affected by decisions for their input when they make decisions? Are decisions made cooperatively? When? By whom? What kind of decisions? Consider where and under what conditions participation occurs now and explore ways to strengthen and encourage those practices. This assessment will help you discern where the weak and strong points are in your company. You will then be in a better position to decide how best to develop more participation in ways appropriate to your company. This assessment may be performed through surveys, small group meetings, focus groups, or informally. Some companies hire professional consultants to move the process forward.

Step 6: Planning for a More Formal System

The steering committee can then develop a plan for the formal approach to participative managing. There are many different models of participation from which to choose. Most revolve around a few basic concepts:

1. *Functional teams:* These are small groups of employees within the same work area who meet periodically to review operations and make recommendations to management.

2. *Self-managing teams:* These are the next step up from functional teams. They actually take over all the supervisory tasks previously assigned to a manager or managers, including quality control, scheduling, work assessment, etc.

3. *Cross-functional teams:* These teams consist of people from different areas who gather to discuss issues where they interact, such as customer service requirements, or company-wide issues, such as safety or leave policy.

4. *Ad-hoc teams:* These are teams assigned to a specific issue. Once the issue is resolved, the team dissolves. Membership usually consists of people appointed by management or the steering committee plus anyone who wants to volunteer.

5. *Job enhancement:* Individual jobs can often be expanded by giving people more leeway to make decisions.

Creating a participation program involves deciding which combination of these vehicles makes sense for your company. Whatever choices are made, however, it is important to reassess them periodically to make sure they meet current needs.

CHAPTER 15

ESOP Case Studies

Corey Rosen

Bimba Manufacturing

If you need a tissue, you might ask for a "Kleenex." If you need a copy, you ask for a "Xerox." If you need a nonrepairable pneumatic actuator (a kind of cylinder), you might well ask for a "Bimba." Bimba Manufacturing is a majority employee-owned, 350-employee manufacturer in Monee, Illinois. The company was started by Charles Bimba. In 1957, Bimba saw a need to produce a cylinder that did not have to be repaired and started manufacturing them. The company grew quickly, branching out into flow control valves, rodless cylinders, linear thrusters, and rotary actuators as well. Their products can be found in applications ranging from automatic scissors to hole-punching machines to robotics.

In 1975, Bimba retired, turning over the company to his son. In 1985, Chuck Bimba decided this was not what he wanted to do the rest of his life. The company was strong, with a young but stable workforce. Selling to an outsider would have been possible, but selling to an ESOP seemed to be a better solution. The Bimba family saw it as the next best thing to passing the business on to another generation.

The strength of the company made financing readily available. A majority ESOP-buyout was almost entirely bank financed. The ESOP replaced a profit sharing plan and was structured in a fairly conventional way. Employees are eligible for participation after six months' service. Allocation of shares is based on relative pay, although there is a small adjustment for years of service.

While Bimba's ESOP structure may be very conventional, its system of management is less so. As Dennis Damrow, Bimba's vice-president for finance puts it, "We have started a journey towards empowerment and participation."

Orientation

The process begins for each new employee with orientation. Bimba's orientation was modeled after that of Web Industries. During a four week process, for one hour each day, new employees meet with someone from a particular area to learn firsthand how that part of the company operates. The process is coordinated by an in-house, volunteer committee. Instructors include managers, work-team leaders, and nonmanagement people. Some of the issues are technical, such as manufacturing and quality. Others focus on the company itself, including finances, history, and business relationships. A third area deals with teamwork, the work ethic, and continuous improvement. Still others focus on wage and benefit issues, including the ESOP. Everyone meets with the president to discuss corporate philosophy.

Brian O'Keefe, an employee owner active in the ESOP process, says the orientation program has helped both get people started on the right foot and turn around people who were cynical. Once current employees are involved in helping to orient new people, their understanding of the company and its objectives becomes much clearer.

Structuring Participation

O'Keefe says that before the ESOP, there were teams, but the teams simply implemented what management told them to do. There were no opportunities for input, and people did not concern themselves with issues between departments.

In 1988, the company was reorganized into three divisions. Supervisors in each division were now required to be coaches; operators were asked to take on more responsibility. Workers were divided into work groups, usually on the basis of common functions. The groups can make decisions or recommendations to management for anything affecting their work, depending on the nature of the issue.

Forming the teams and getting them to work well to solve problems, of course, were two different things. Many supervisors resisted, and some still do. Employees were now being asked to share more ideas and information, but many did not have the necessary skills or training to do so. To help deal with this, each department set up training programs in quality control, problem solving, statistical process control, and other techniques. Employees can take college classes in a variety of skill areas, with tuition reimbursed on a sliding scale according to the course grade (this procedure was based on an employee suggestion).

To help get input from people not on the teams, minutes from all team meetings are posted so that other employees can make suggestions about those issues.

Participation at the Company Level

An ESOP committee was formed with representatives from all three shifts. The committee acts as a voice for employees with management and a source of information about the ESOP, benefits, and corporate finances. During "employee ownership week," employees meet with the president to ask any questions about any topic.

This year, the committee is arranging a full-voting seat for a non-management person on the board of directors. The committee also decided that committee members would not be eligible to serve. A primary was held in which 24 people ran. The field was narrowed to three, and a toolmaker with 10-years' seniority was selected.

Participation also extends to profits through Bimba's profit-based bonus system.

Results

Since the ESOP, Bimba's stock has doubled in value, a 50,000 square foot addition was added, scrap has fallen, profits are up, employment is up 40%, sales have almost doubled, new products are being introduced faster, and a facility in Great Britain has opened. Bimba has clearly come a long way in its journey.

King Arthur Flour

ESOPs tend to be set up in well-established companies, but there probably are not any that are more established than King Arthur Flour, a 207-year old operation. For 205 of those years, the company was entirely family owned, selling flour to various markets around the country. During the 1970s, a new generation began to expand the company. Through a number of acquisitions, King Arthur grew from a small single-product operation to New England's largest bakery-supply distributor, employing 150 people. It supplied virtually every ingredient used by bakers, as well as manufacturing pie fillings, jams, jellies, flavorings, and ice cream toppings. By 1984, a change in corporate philosophy led the company to focus on flour and shift most operations to outsourcing contractors. It sold off the acquisitions, relocated to Rutland, Vermont, and shrunk down to four people.

The contracting-out approach worked, and by 1990 the number of employees had grown to 12. The company increased its sales of flour in the Northeast through supermarkets and other retail outlets and brought back in-house the sale of 50- and 100-pound bags of flour to bakeries. Also in that year, the company decided to start a mail order division to handle sales to individuals who had moved out of the Northeast and could no longer purchase King Arthur flour at their supermarket. The catalog grew dramatically, spawned a retail-outlet store in Vermont, and expanded distribution of supermarket flour to the rest of the country. By 1997, employment had grown to 90.

Over the years, the company had a number of opportunities to sell, but the family retained a preference to staying independent. The upcoming generation, however, lacked a strong interest in running the business. Inside the company, a culture was developing where employees were increasingly asked to act like owners. Providing real ownership was a logical next step. An ESOP seemed to fit well, providing ownership to employees and liquidity to the selling shareholders over the 10- to 15-year time horizon they had set to sell their interests.

Plan Design and Structure

Several design issues had to be decided before the plan could be started. A leveraged approach was chosen, but the loan money came entirely from company cash. An outside team of consultants set up the plan, charging $30,000 for its implementation. While employees were kept appraised of the progress of the plan from early on, the selling family, the vice president for finance, and the vice president for human resources ultimately composed the internal design team. When the ESOP plan document was completed, all the employees met to hear a presentation on it and to discuss the plan's future.

Then there was the question of fairness. In many ESOPs, people considered key to the company are given options or other ownership opportunities to supplement what the ESOP provides. That seemed inconsistent with the company's culture, however, so ownership will only come through the ESOP. A related fairness issue is providing stock for new employees after the loan is repaid. While this is a long time off, King Arthur is already looking at ways to keep everyone an owner.

Creating an Ownership Culture

Since 1992, the company has been practicing open-book management. The company has quarterly company-wide meetings (and monthly division meetings) to go over the financials and ESOP issues. All employees are trained to read the income statements and balance sheets, starting with the difference between sales and profit, and moving to more detailed descriptions relevant to each employee's area. For instance, employees learn why $20,000 of warehouse racking doesn't show up on the income statement in the month it is purchased, where it goes on the balance sheet, how it is depreciated, and what happens if it is sold.

More important, however, is explaining to people what their critical numbers are, the numbers that drive the success of the various aspects of the company's operations. The company has a phone-orders group for its catalog operation, for instance, whose critical numbers include "upselling" customers additional products related to those they are ordering. The impact of these additional sales on overhead absorption is carefully reviewed. Employee teams meet regularly to go over the numbers and talk about ideas to improve operations. The reward of the business game is profit sharing, currently paid annually, but soon to be upgraded to quarterly. To make ownership more immediate to people, the profit-sharing bonus will eventually be paid based on the number of shares an individual has in the ESOP.

The company has been very successful since the ESOP was set up and has been able to declare substantial dividends to help repay the loan. In fact, allocations are running about half of total compensation. Despite this and the participative open-book style, the company still has a ways to go before people really understand the long-term benefits of ownership, something management hopes the stock-based bonus will help clarify. On the other hand, the plan has already helped people understand how the company's four divisions work together. Given its commitment to what research shows are "all the right moves," it seems likely that ownership will in fact become a very important part of the King Arthur culture.

McKay Nursery

"We never thought what we were doing was a big deal; it always just seemed like common sense to us." That's how Griff Mason, president of McKay Nurseries in Waterloo, Wisconsin, described his reaction to McKay's being named a winner of a "Business Enterprise Trust Award" in 1997. The awards are given annually to four U.S. businesses or business leaders for "exemplary acts of courage, integrity, and social vision in business." Each year, the NCEO is asked to nominate companies; this year we nominated McKay. The award has been given for several years. Other NCEO members who have won include Rick Surpin of Community Health Care Associates, Gun Denhardt of Hannah Anderson, and Jack Stack of SRC Holdings. Winners meet with the President, are the subjects of Harvard Business School Case Studies, and get considerable national attention. Given all this acclaim, McKay's common sense may in fact be rather extraordinary.

McKay is the tenth largest regional nursery in the U.S., selling both as a retailer and on a wholesale basis, mostly to landscape architects. While many people may not think of Wisconsin as a place where there would be large numbers of Hispanic migrant workers, McKay and many other Wisconsin agricultural operations (such as Green Giant), rely heavily on migrant labor. Over 100 migrant employees work for McKay, generally for an eight-month season. What makes McKay unusual is the way it treats its migrant employees. It wants them to come back every year, and a stunning 90% do. They come back because McKay treats them very well, so well that Maria Nichols, director of Wisconsin's migrant workers' program, says that McKay is the standard her department would like to see other Wisconsin employers achieve. The workers get good housing, fair wages (the company paid migrants overtime wages long before it was legally required), excellent training, and, perhaps most important, they are included in McKay's ESOP. With contributions to the ESOP often at the legal maximum, and with McKay having grown 400% since the ESOP was set up in 1984, migrant workers with 20- to 25-years' seniority will probably accumulate six-figure accounts.

The impact of this is striking. The average migrant worker has 15 years' seniority. Some have become full-time supervisory personnel. People have been able to buy their own houses and send their children to college. But it is not just money. In a tape made for the awards (narrated by Bill Moyers), McKay employee-owner Jose Rodriguez says, "we give our best to make things better because we see it not just belonging to one person but to all migrants." In short, McKay is providing dignity at work to people who do not often get it.

Mason is quick to point out, however, that this is not simply an act of altruism. McKay's employee-centered philosophy results in loyal, well-trained, highly motivated people. The 400% growth since the ESOP was set up is ample testimony that treating people well has been a very good business practice.

Company History

The company was founded in 1897 to buy and sell fruit trees from farm to farm. Later, it moved into decorative plants and, after World War II, began offering plants to landscape designers. By the 1980s, landscaping became the primary business of the company. Most nurseries were small and local; McKay was unusual in its size and scope of services.

McKay's progressive labor policies go back many years. For instance, it set up a retirement plan for employees in 1961, something almost unheard of in the industry at that time. In 1968, a profit-sharing plan was set up. Free housing for migrant employees that exceeded state standards was set up from the outset. Migrant laborers were also allowed to take unpaid days off.

Selling to the ESOP

In 1984, McKay's over 70-year old president, Karl Junginger, was looking for a way to sell his ownership interest, as were three other top people.

Unfortunately, every sale option could have potentially resulted in the company relocating to a major urban area. There was discussion of management buying out the company, but that involved too much debt and risk for them. ESOPs were not well known at the time, but when McKay's managers became aware of this approach, their dilemma seemed solved. There were already substantial assets in the profit-sharing plan that could help finance the transaction, making the large purchase more manageable. Employees were asked if they were willing to loan some of the assets in the plan to the ESOP. One-half of the assets were loaned. In addition, the four major sellers made personal guarantees on the bank loan for the ESOP. McKay became a 100% ESOP company.

In each ensuing year, McKay set performance records. It paid off its debt to the profit-sharing plan in five years and the bank loan five years later. By any standard, McKay has been the kind of company that makes the entire employee ownership community very proud.

MPD, Inc.

You've probably never heard of MPD, but you probably do know someone who wishes no one had heard of them. That's because, amongst other things, MPD makes breathalyzers and speed checking equipment, such as radar guns and the signs on highways that tell you how fast you are going. The 413-employee company also manufactures electronic components for commercial and military uses. It has 310 employees in the U.S. at its Owensboro, Kentucky, operation, 100 in the United Kingdom, and three in Singapore. The Owensboro division is unionized.

Since starting its ESOP in 1997, MPD has taken one of the most comprehensive approaches to developing an ownership culture we have yet seen, one that can serve as a template for other new ESOPs.

Origins of the Plan

MPD started as Ken-Rad, a maker of lamps and tubes. In 1945, GE bought the company, but had to divest it in 1986 when another GE acquisition made them a 100% monopoly in a segment of the electronic component business. That transaction was completed in 1987, when investors bought 74% of the company (the rest was bought by 55 other individuals, including some managers), and renamed it MPD, Inc. The company subsequently acquired other operations, including those making the breathalyzers and speed measurement equipment. The investors planned to sell in several years, but the stock grew quickly, and they held on to it for ten years. Other buyers were willing to buy divisions of the company, but not the whole company. That could lead to job loss, so the owners decided in 1997 to sell to an ESOP instead.

The transaction was an unusually complicated one, involving a tender offer to the 56 owners, 49 of whom sold 97% of the company to the ESOP. Both the company and the ESOP had a full set of financial and legal advisors. Financing included both a bank loan and notes back to the sellers. The plan initially covered all U.S. salaried employees. Including the union employees at the outset would mean reopening the contract, but after the ESOP was completed, union members were added.

Announcing and Overseeing the Plan

Three and a half months into the process of putting the purchase together, management met with all salaried employees at a local college to tell them about the ESOP. The next day, they told the union people that they would bring them into the ESOP after the transaction closed. Then they met with all employees in groups of 10 or fewer. They hired Ownership Development, Inc. to design a formal training program for all employees, consisting of 20 one-day sessions of 15 people each on team building, understanding financials, how the ESOP works, and other issues. Any questions not answered at each meeting by the trainers were answered by management at the end of the day.

The plan is governed by a directed outside trustee. The trustee is directed by a voting committee of three managers. An administrative ESOP committee made up of two senior managers and two non-management employees oversees plan operations. Finally a participation committee consisting of nine elected employees and one manager handles communication and participation issues.

Participation

At the first annual meeting (held at the local performing arts center), reports from each subsidiary were presented and financials were reviewed. The trustee made a presentation in connection with the first ESOP statement. In a particularly innovative step, the board meeting was held in front of everyone, with a narrator describing what was going on.

Brown-bag lunches are held monthly where people report on financial, product, and other business developments. A periodic ESOP newsletter is published to provide additional details.

Employees are divided into 32 teams. Each team picks one to four goals related to its work area that can improve EBITDA (earnings before interest, taxes, depreciation, and amortization). Rationales for the choices are presented at the brown-bag lunches. Progress towards the goals is posted on big posters around the company and discussed at the lunches. The human resources department "Blood, Sweat, and Tears" team, for instance, picked turnover, medical costs, and compliance costs as their key measures. A benchmark was established by choosing a prior measurement period to beat.

For all the teams, "smiley" and "frownee" faces are pasted on each progress report to indicate at a glance how the team is doing. A bonus will be paid based on an overall EBITDA budget, and charts let everyone know the progress towards that objective.

MPD's CEO Gary Braswell says that employee behavior has not changed yet, but he knows that the process takes time. Having non-U.S. employees is also a challenge; they currently do not participate in an ownership plan.

While change may not have occurred yet, there is good reason to think it will. The MPD approach embodies many of the key lessons of creating ownership cultures. Employees can set their own goals, but they are well-justified business goals. Participation does not exist for its own sake, but is linked to specific business needs. Short- and long-term compensation focuses people on profit and growth. People get the information they need, and are taught to use it. In short, the MPD program is one of the best designed starts to an ESOP we have seen.

Phelps County Bank

When you walk into Phelps County Bank, it looks like an ordinary bank in an ordinary small, Midwestern town. But Phelps County Bank in Rolla, Missouri is far from ordinary. It is now close to 100% owned by an ESOP, one of the few majority-owned banks in the country, and has a very participative management style. By 1990, Phelps' employee owners helped the company's stock grow 411% since the ESOP was started in 1980 and saw its assets grow from $20 million to $87 million. By contrast, over that 10-year period of endemic banking problems, its two competitors, both owned by large holding companies, saw their stock go up 211% in one case and decline 12% in the other. Although the three banks were close in size, Phelps grabbed over half the new loans in three years and over 40% of the new accounts.

Making the ESOP Matter

Phelps started its ESOP in 1980 by buying 8% of the shares from its owner, Don Castleman. But Emma Lou Brent, Phelps' CEO, did not see much change in employee attitudes. Along the way, she had read results of an NCEO study indicating that people really only get excited about ownership if they receive substantial annual contributions. So she decided the company would need to find a way to increase its employee ownership.

In 1986, the ESOP was leveraged to buy enough stock to bring it from 13% to 32% of the company. Employees would now be getting 25% or more of pay contributed to the ESOP annually (30% in 1990, thanks to dividends on the shares). Salaries were already 20% above competition. The increased costs, Brent told employees, would have to be paid for by improved performance. The plan worked. After years of steady, but slow, growth, Phelps' stock doubled over the next four years. In 1991, Castleman was ready to sell more stock, and the ESOP was leveraged again to bring total ownership to 68%.

Employee ownership over 25% brings particular problems in the banking industry. ESOPs are considered holding companies, adding another layer of regulation. Although a hassle, Brent says the problems can be solved and are well worth the motivation substantial ownership brings.

Training to Be Owners

While most banks do employee training, Phelps has an especially extensive program. Each new employee is assigned a mentor to help her learn the system. In addition to training for specific jobs, all employees are trained in selling, because Brent believes that every owner's job is to sell the bank's services. Company ethics require that customers are not sold things they do not need, but everyone tries to sell the services that can be useful.

While Phelps' employees have many rights and benefits, the culture of the company is demanding. People are expected to make a contribution, to work together, and to think of ways to improve service. All employees receive regular performance appraisals, and, at the suggestion of an employee, an "upward-appraisal" system was initiated to review supervisors.

In addition, Brent has held breakfast meetings with small groups of employees to go over the bank's financial situation, the ESOP, and other matters. Each year, the company sends people to NCEO's "Just for Employees" conference, selecting a winner based on the best new idea. One year, the winner was a 25-page business plan by a customer-service representative proposing the bank sell annuities to its customers. The idea generated over $10,000 in additional fees in just its first few months. The annual competition has now been expanded to provide more prizes for more winners.

Getting Employees Involved

Brent herself started as a part-time teller and knew that employees had a lot of good ideas and valuable information to share. The trick was to find ways to encourage employee owners to share what they knew. Phelps started its ESOP in 1980, but it was not until 1986, when the ESOP moved up to 32% of the shares and a new employee-involvement program started, that its ESOP really took off.

In 1989, Phelps set up a formal participation program through what it called a "problem-buster" committee. Six employees with diverse roles and approaches were put on the committee to review suggestions or problems employees knew needed to be solved. Committee members were appointed by the bank's executive committee.

The problem-buster committee met monthly to review suggestions and problems raised by any of the bank's employees. It made recommendations to the executive committee, which normally approved the proposals. The committee could also put out "problem alerts" to solicit employee input. If the suggestion could be implemented immediately, supervisors were simply asked to handle them; if not, the committee sought volunteers to serve on ad hoc problem-solving committees. The volunteers received small prizes, like a dinner for two, when they finished the job. The problem-buster committee then screened the recommendations. A monthly memo distributed to all employees reviewed committee actions.

Maintaining Participation

Companies often start employee-involvement programs with great enthusiasm and fanfare. The programs work for a while, but often lose effectiveness if not constantly re-evaluated and renewed. Phelps' problem-buster committee worked so well that it lost much of its value. People became so accustomed to sharing ideas and information that they were discussing and resolving problems before they were ever raised to the committee. The committee had helped employees create the habit of thinking about and resolving problems both individually and in teams. Once that habit was established, it created an opportunity to develop more extensive means of involvement.

The new system at Phelps has several key features:

- *Teams:* Employees are divided up into teams to deal with various functional areas at the bank. Membership is based on appropriate expertise, but all meetings are open to anyone from any other team.

- *E-mail:* E-mail has become a critical part of the company's communication process. Everyone is on the system and can address an individual or a group of people very easily. A daily e-mail newsletter called "Bits and Pieces" keeps people up to date on news of the bank; board reports are also available.

- *Empowerment and training:* As at many companies, employees are given more individual responsibility to deal with issues themselves. The empowerment program works in large part because of the extensive training employees receive. American Institute of Banking programs held in the area are attended mostly by Phelps employees. Employees are taught to read financial statements from the

bank. Half the employee owners recently completed a course to begin a Certified Financial Planning Degree. Employees are sent to
seminars and conferences on all aspects of banking. Bank special
promotions are preceded by extensive education. Phelps is also
embarking on a program to cross-train employees so that employees are better able to serve customers and so that jobs can be covered when employees are absent.

- *EARS (Error Alert Response):* EARS is one of the most creative Phelps
  innovations. In 1992, when empowerment was started, management
  decided that when employees did make important decisions to solve
  customer problems, other employees needed to know about it. So
  EARS was created to use e-mail to make this possible. For example,
  a customer calls to ask why she received an overdue notice. An employee owner discovers the reason was an early automatic payment
  drafted from her account due to a holiday weekend. The employee
  tells the customer what has happened and that the bank will refund
  the overdraft charge. Now the employee describes what has happened via e-mail so that other employees can be alert to this issue.

- *Committee minutes:* Minutes for all committee meetings are kept and
  then are sent out via e-mail. Given their added responsibilities, employees need to know what is happening in all aspects of the bank.
  At most banks, tellers are not responsible for explaining how a
  bank's new CD policy works or how annuities can help plan for retirement, for instance. At Phelps, employee owners are expected to
  know:

- *Mentoring:* All new employees are assigned a buddy to help them
  understand the ESOP and the bank. For instance, after the annual
  shareholder meeting (which all employees attend), a buddy will help
  the new employee go over the ESOP account statement line by line.

- *Learning by games:* When there is new information to learn, the company often institutes a game to make it fun. For instance, all financial information is available to everyone on their computer. To help
  employees understand the various ratios and other numbers involved, Phelps created a "Wheel of Fortune" game. Employees were
  divided into teams and prizes awarded to everyone, winners and los-
  ers alike.

- *Goal-setting meetings:* All teams engage in regular goal setting to establish measurements for feedback on how they are doing. Team goals then form the basis for corporate goal-setting meetings. The corporate goals then go back down to the teams, who then incorporate them into their objectives.

The Payoff

Ownership and participation have paid off in many ways. Managers can focus on what they do best, letting employees handle many matters management normally handles. Employees are enthused about the chance to have a say. And everyone is excited about the financial payoff. By 1991, on average, a typical 10-year employee had an account balance of $40,000, enough to buy a typical house in Rolla, and in 1990 received 45% of pay in contributions, dividends, and stock appreciation.

In 1994, the ESOP owns close to 100% of the stock. ESOP contributions have been at 25% of pay, even though other staff compensation remains higher than that of competitors. Yet Phelps has been able to more than pay for these added costs with the profits its employee owners have helped create. The bank's stock has increased more than fivefold since the ESOP's inception, about double that of the nearest competitor. In 1993, between the bank's ESOP contribution and appreciation on existing balances, the typical Phelps employee saw an ESOP account balance growth equal to 75% of pay. The rest of the banking industry should pay attention.

Reflexite Corporation

The Reflexite Corporation was founded in 1970 by two brothers who are both engineers. The company, which is located in New Britain, Connecticut, develops and manufactures reflective material for many uses. There are now 106 employees. The company is privately held. There is a nine-member board of directors, five of whom are outsiders.

Reflexite set up its ESOP in 1985. The company made its first contribution in November of that year. The ESOP has been combined with a defined benefit pension plan. This creates a "floor effect" that insures that if the ESOP stock value falls below a certain level, the pension plan guarantees the level of payment any worker would have received under the pension plan. In other words, workers have the opportunity to be better off at pay out but cannot be worse off.

We asked Cecil Ursprung, president of Reflexite, to tell us about why his company established an ESOP and what advice he would give to others considering this step. Mr. Ursprung and Reflexite demonstrate the three characteristics we found in our research of over 40 companies to be the most important in creating owners who are satisfied with their jobs and committed to their organizations. Those characteristics are (1) making a sizable contribution to the ESOP, (2) demonstrating a sincere commitment to the idea of employee ownership by management, and (3) communicating with employees about their ownership.

Q. *Why did you set up your plan?*

A.   There were a number of reasons. Let me just go through them with you. First, the ESOP allows our founders/principal owners to phase out their involvement in the ownership and management of the company over the time period that they choose. They had outside offers but chose to sell to the ESOP because they believed that the company could achieve most by remaining independent, had a strong commitment to the community, and felt that the company's unique technology, and thus their jobs, would be saved.

The owners had watched what had happened to other local businesses once they were sold to absentee owners who ran them by looking at the bottom line. Return on equity and stock value are the two major criteria for assessing a business by non-community owners. If those fail to meet the standards set for them, the business is often milked and closed with no thought to the effect on the workers and community. The owners did not want this to happen at Reflexite.

The next reason for setting up the ESOP was a philosophical one. Several years ago the board of directors established as a corporate objective providing a means for all the employees to share in the success of the company. The ESOP provides that means.

The third reason is a practical one. Our competitors are much larger than we are and have greater resources. We felt that providing stock ownership to the employees would be a motivator. We also felt that the

ESOP would help us attract and retain top employees. Having the ESOP as an incentive will contribute to overall satisfaction and thus encourage them to stay with us. We think we see this happening already.

Fourth, the ESOP determined a value and created a market for the stock of the present stockholders. At present the principle owners have no plans to leave the company. However, they would like to revert back more to their original roles of entrepreneurs rather than the management ones that they have had to take over the years. They would both like to work more on the research and development aspect of the business. They feel that their impact on the technology would be a greater contribution.

Fifth, we think that the ESOP will contribute to increased productivity and profitability. And we see some indications of that already. I overheard one employee saying, "I guess I better watch my personal phone calls since I'm the owner here now." Employees do seem to be watching how money is spent and are more attuned to waste. Peer pressure plays a role here.

Sixth, establishing the ESOP will help smooth out the management and ownership succession of the company.

And lastly, an ESOP does provide some strong financial incentives for a company. We had been looking at various ways to accomplish some of the measures talked about above. After passage of the 1984 ESOP legislation we decided this is it. The ESOP is a perfect match for our needs.

Q. *How did you find out about the ESOP?*

A. The ESOP has had its share of the business press in the last four or five years. Along about late 1983 or early 1984, I read an article that encouraged me to look into this idea more. This resulted in my being put in touch with two local companies which had ESOPs. Then as I traveled around the country I would get in touch with practitioners in the field, who did plan design or communications programs, and made appointments to speak with them. I read and read on the subject and reported my findings to the owners and the board. Everything we found out encouraged us to continue along this course. In June 1984, we had a practitioner come and give an educational program to the board. We all felt satisfied that this vehicle would help us achieve many of our goals, practical and philosophical.

Q. *What advice would you give to anyone considering setting up a plan?*

A. First, I would recommend that you become conversant with the ESOP and related matters, not your lawyer, not your accountant, but you. This is so you know what you are getting and what your options are. This is a complicated endeavor with involvement with ERISA (the 1974 law governing retirement security), the Department of Labor, and the IRS. It is not a pension plan. Your insurance person or your actuary cannot tell you all the facts. Get involved every step of the way. This is a permanent thing and can have a major impact on your company.

Second, I would say that you should hire *experienced* legal and appraisal people. Don't let somebody learn at your expense. And most importantly, make sure your philosophy about the ESOP and that of the people you hire to help implement the plan match. If you want the plan solely for the tax benefits or to use for estate planning, fine. However, if achieving the potential of the ESOP as a management philosophy and as a good way to run a business is your goal, then let that insure the choices you make about the plan. Don't let anybody else tell you what your philosophy should be.

Third, get your employees involved early. Begin to talk about it with your employees. When we decided here that this is the way we wanted to go, we told our employees. We told them we have studied this concept; we might still yet find some legal or technical thing which might make it impossible for us to do it, but the way it looks now, we are going to do this. You might run the risk of raising expectations. However, if you go through the whole thing and then spring it on them, human nature dictates, they are going to be suspicious.

Fourth, join the support organizations. If there is more than one, investigate. If they serve different purposes then join both. It's not very expensive, and it's worth it.

Fifth, do not sell the ESOP as a retirement plan. The reason for this is that unless an employee is in his mid-50s or so, this will mean nothing. It will be a zero motivator to those people in their 20s and 30s. Nobody thinks about retirement then. Sell it as ownership in the organization, which it is. People will respond to that. If they know the amount they get in their accounts results directly from how well the company does, which rests on how well they perform, they will act like they own the company.

And sixth, but not any less important than my previous recommendations, is to seek out and talk to other business people about this. Find out what their experiences have been. They can tell you things that no practitioner, no academic, and no organization can.

Reflexite Corporation Five Years Later

"I can speak for all the stockholders and all the board members: we have had more fun and we have made more money than we ever could by selling to someone else." These comments were made by Cecil Ursprung in 1991 at the NCEO annual meeting. In 1983, Ursprung had just been hired as the new president of Reflexite. Four days before he was supposed to start working, he attended a special board meeting. It seemed that a Fortune 500 competitor had offered to buy the company for an astounding 42 times earnings. Ursprung argued that he believed that everyone could "have more fun and make more money" if they did not sell. Reflexite turned down the offer from the large company as well as five other offers over the next eight months.

In 1984, a new course was chosen instead. An ESOP would be installed to provide liquidity for the current owners, to reward and attract employees, and to form the basis for a more participative, and, hopefully, productive work environment. There was also a strong commitment to keeping the company and jobs in New Britain.

Initially, the plan bought just 1% of the stock, using excess funds from a terminated defined benefit plan. The company used the ESOP as part of a "floor-offset" plan, an approach that guaranteed that employees would get at least as much as the defined benefit plan promised, but could get more if the ESOP shares performed better than necessary to meet this minimum (new floor offset plans have since been disallowed).

At the same time, the company put a moratorium on new offers. It is likely the offers would have kept flowing. Reflexite had developed a technology that produced exceptionally bright reflective material, much brighter than anything else on the market. From bicyclists to astronauts, people have developed a strong loyalty to the extra measure of safety these devices provide.

Creating an Ownership Culture

Reflexite's technology alone, however, would not allow it to meet Ursprung's challenge of "having more fun and making more money" than by selling to someone else. After all, other people would pay handsomely for the technology, as demonstrated by all the offers to buy. Reflexite's employee owners would have to show that they could do better with the technology than even a giant (and very successful giant) Fortune 500 company could.

To do that, Reflexite embarked on creating an ownership culture. As Ursprung points out, "embark" is the right word. Like walking toward a rainbow, the ultimate goal always seemed on the horizon, no matter how far along the journey people had come. There were several components involved. In 1988, the ESOP was leveraged to 31% (it now owns 35%); the company is committed to eventual substantial majority ownership by the ESOP. In addition, 50 of the company's 270 employees have bought 28% of the shares individually. That made employee ownership significant enough to get people's financial attention.

The ESOP provided long-term financial rewards, but Ursprung believed short-term rewards were needed as well. Part of this comes from passing through dividends to employees—averaging over $1,000 per employee in 1990. A second element is the owner's bonus. The company contributes 3% of monthly operating profits to a pool, which is divided by participants according to the number of ESOP shares in their account. Between bonuses, dividends, and the ESOP contribution, variable pay constitutes up to 30% of total payroll. Of all of the companies we have studied, Reflexite has one of the highest rates of variable to fixed pay.

All of this made employees into owners in the financial sense, but did not automatically translate into an ownership culture in day-to-day work. For that, employees needed to get more involved in making decisions. So in 1988, Reflexite passed through voting rights. "You have to have enough faith and trust in the people you work with to pass through the vote," Ursprung told the NCEO meeting. So far, Ursprung says, that faith and trust has been well justified.

Passing through voting rights, however, was the easy part. "Participation in decisions that affect people's jobs has been much more difficult to achieve," Ursprung said. "It requires constant effort. The further we get into it, the further we have to go." One approach is a new Quality Improvement Process. Employees are being trained in problem-solving techniques and participative skills so that they can work as teams to create their own solutions. The company also provides financial statements to employees, along with explanations for each line item.

Results

For competitive reasons, the company is reluctant to have financial results discussed in print, but suffice it to say that the Fortune 500 company offer turned out to be far too low in light of what the employee owners have been able to achieve on their own. By any standard, the company has been an extraordinary success.

The secrets are simple common sense, says Ursprung: "The more you treat people like owners, the more they tend to act like owners. The more you share power through participation and the more you share financial rewards, the more there is of power and financial rewards to go around for everyone." It seems Reflexite's owners really are making more money and (Ursprung actually put this first) having more fun.

Scot Forge

It's easy to find a Scot Forge employee at a conference. They're the ones in the red tartan plaid clothing, just one of many traditions at Scot. Founded in 1893 as a small hammer shop in Chicago, today it is a 100% ESOP-owned manufacturer of custom open die and rolled ring forgings located in Spring Grove, IL, Franklin Park, IL, and Clinton, WI.

Iron forging is hard work, but the company's over 500 employees enjoy both an unusually participative culture and pro-employee environment. That helped Scot become the first North American open die shop to become ISO 9002 certified and to increase employment over the last twenty years by 250%.

Roots of the Ownership Culture

Scot had been a successful family owned business when it started its ESOP in 1978 to provide liquidity for the owners. The company became 100% employee owned in 1997 and then became an S corporation. Setting up an ESOP was only the first step to becoming a company of owners. Until around 1990, most of the decision making had been top-down. But ownership cultures get created by giving employees more of a role in making decisions about their jobs and more information about how to do them well. Scot's CEO realized the company's structure wasn't doing enough along these lines.

So he decided to bring in a continuous improvement team coach to create and mentor employee teams. The first team was to prepare for a big conference they were hosting by making the plant presentable for the gathering. The coach appointed several forge workers to the housekeeping team. The workers weren't thrilled with the idea of going out to scrub the plant, but they got out their brooms and garbage cans and went at it. Unfortunately, as soon as they cleaned things up, they got dirty again. The team was a total flop. Its goals were hard to measure, the means to achieve it ambiguous, and the task never-ending.

Getting Teams to Work

But management didn't give up. They did some research on their own and set up new teams. The first really successful team came from an employee idea. Employees in the saw shop formed their own team to see why their area was producing an unusual number of complaints from customers that their products didn't conform to the specifications they needed. They found the problem wasn't operator error, it was a saw that was out of adjustment. They fixed the saw and solved the problem. No manager was involved.

Management quickly learned that if teams were going to work, employees needed to buy in. If employees identified the problems themselves, rather than management just saying "you're going to be on this team to solve this problem," things worked a lot better. After the saw team success, lots of employees had ideas. One team in the machine shop decided they needed an inventory control room to catalogue supplies appropriately. They researched it, figured out how much it would cost to staff and equip, and what it would save.

Another team—a safety team called COGS (Communicating On Getting Safer)—looked at how many accidents they had. They hired an outside firm to come in to advise them and went for training to learn how to observe what was happening on the plant floor and how to give feedback so people could accept their observations. Then each trained employee took aside two others and trained them. Now they have a whole company of safety observes. All employees are trained and take turns each month to observe safety practices and provide feedback. The team reduced lost time due to accidents by 2,400 hours in the first four months, injuries 22%, and lost-time injuries by 35%. Over a full-year period, their accident rate was 42% lower. Since everyone at Scot is on salary, avoiding lost-time accidents saves a lot of money.

Team Training and Structure

To make teams work well, employees learn about group process. Groups identify specific, obtainable goals, not like "make the place look cleaner," a goal that can never be fully measured or accomplished. After groups have tackled a project, there is a feedback process to figure out what worked.

The teams work on paid time, although sometimes they find they need to work after working hours on a voluntary basis. Some teams are ongoing (like safety), while others are ad-hoc, one-issue groups. Of course, sometimes it is management that identifies a problem. Creating effective teams is tougher then. Management will choose some team members from different areas for specific skills, as well as asking for volunteers. The process still works, but more effort is required to make sure it does.

Teams are only part of the ownership culture at Scot. Financial information is shared in an understandable way and in detail on a regular basis. Monthly meetings give people a chance to learn about developments in the company. Extensive communications through a variety of media help keep people informed.

Employees are noticeable at ESOP meetings by their numbers, not just their jackets. But the teams have been the key to making Scot an exemplar of what employee ownership can be.

This case study is based on the remarks of Karen York, a staff accountant at Scot Forge, at an NCEO annual conference.

Smith and Company

In 1993, Sam Smith was beginning to feel a little weary of being president of his 22-employee civil engineering firm, Smith and Company. The Poplar Bluff, Missouri, business was stable and successful, working with environmental projects and helping to build infrastructure projects: including bridges, highways, airports, water, and wastewater systems. Smith started the company in 1965. He now felt it might be time to sell part or all of his ownership interests.

That year, he attended an NCEO ESOP seminar in Memphis. The idea intrigued him, both because of its tax and financial benefits, but also because he liked the idea of turning his company over to his employees. One of the companies mentioned as an example was Springfield ReManufacturing Corporation (SRC) in Springfield, Missouri, a company gaining national attention for developing the "Great Game of Business" concept. Smith arranged to meet with Tom Samsel at SRC (Samsel heads the ESOP Committee at SRC and is an NCEO board member). What was scheduled as a brief meeting turned into a long one as Samsel explained what the ESOP and the Great Game approach had accomplished for SRC and its employee owners. By the time he left, Smith was convinced that both ideas would make a lot of sense at his company.

Putting the ESOP in Place

In 1994, Smith installed the ESOP, using it to borrow enough money to buy 30% of the company with a five-year note. Installation costs were modest, well below the $15,000 to $25,000 or more ESOPs usually cost. Part of the savings came from working with a local bank that was enthusiastic about the company and the ESOP idea, and that had ESOP experience. The bank waived many of the normal legal fees involved in processing the loan, fees that often can add $10,000 or more to transaction costs. While such waivers are not the norm, ESOP advisors report that companies with strong credit appeal to lenders can sometimes reduce or eliminate lender costs, especially if the bank has enough experience with these loans to prepare the needed legal opinions in-house.

The ESOP that resulted is conventionally structured, with allocation based on pay, graduated vesting starting after three years and increasing to 100% after seven, and pass-through voting only on major corporate issues. Distributions for terminated employees begin at the end of the plan year employees leave. The ESOP replaced a profit-sharing plan, with ESOP contributions pegged at a much higher level than the predecessor plan.

Playing the Game

Getting the ESOP installed turned out to be a fairly painless process. The next step, making ownership part of the corporate culture, required more work. Smith started meeting weekly with managers, who then met with line employees in small groups to discuss business and ESOP issues. Each month, there is also a company-wide meeting to discuss any business issues people want to cover.

In addition, at voluntary monthly Tuesday and Wednesday night sessions, the financial statements are reviewed. About 60% to 75% of the employees show up. At first, Smith led the meetings himself. That had "zero credibility," he reported. Smith felt hurt that people with whom he had worked for a long time were skeptical. So he assigned five people at random to figure out how to do it better. They met with the firm's outside CPA, then picked one person to give the presentation. Now different volunteers make the presentation at different meetings. That has provided great credibility and has assured that a number of people now understand the financials well enough to explain them. People never learn as well, after all, as when they have to teach.

The meetings have provided people with a chance to give input. To reward the fruits of that effort, a profit-sharing plan was created, the "bigger bucket plan." A profit target is set, and when the "bucket" is filled, 25% is distributed to employees. When they achieve a goal, they make a point of celebrating and inviting the press. The resulting publicity has helped increase people's interest. There are also specific incentive games for various groups, such as improving accounts receivable.

Results

The introduction of the ESOP was not without its difficulties. Some engineers left the company because they wanted to concentrate solely on engineering, rather than focusing on business as well. Smith also thought the initial valuation was too low, although not low enough to discourage him from going forward.

Overall, the results have been impressive. The original ESOP loan bought 30% of the company. Scheduled as a five-year loan, it was paid off in two; an additional loan will be taken out this year to buy 30% more. Since the plan was set up, employment has grown from 22 to 36 and the value of the business has doubled, meaning Smith's 70% ownership is worth 40% more than his 100% ownership was worth two years ago. As Tom Samsel would point out, Smith is not only making more money, but he's having more fun as well.

SRC Holdings

Imagine walking onto a factory floor and listening to a machine operator tell you about the impact of scrap on profits before tax, or about why Wal-Mart's price-to-earnings ratio is 56 to 1. It happened to this writer walking around and talking randomly to people at SRC Holdings Corporation (SRC) in Springfield, Missouri.

The SRC story is now a familiar one in the employee ownership community, thanks to continuing national publicity. In 1983, Jack Stack and 12 other managers bought the struggling division of International Harvester, putting up $100,000 in cash and borrowing $8.9 million (Stack says the only way they got the money is that the bank made a mistake). SRC's 171 employees were soon brought into ownership through an ESOP, which now owns about one-third of the company. Today, SRC employs over 900 people. Its stock has increased in value from $.10 per share to $84.00 per share. It did this through what it calls the "Great Game of Business." The game has three key components: sharing detailed financial information, paying bonuses based on "critical numbers," and getting employees involved in day-to-day decisions.

Sharing the Financials

A lot of companies now share financial data with employees. SRC inundates people with data. Each week at the "Great Huddle," Stack, managers, and any employee who wants to attend go over detailed projections of sales, profits, shipments, and other key data, matching them against actual performance. Few people who do not need to be there show up. After all, they could be working to earn income. The rapid fire meeting only stops when there is a discrepancy—for better or worse. SRC does not like surprises. The managers then meet with employees to go over the numbers and to develop numbers for the next projections. Employees all have access to a 120-page monthly financial statement, and most read and understand, at least the part applying to their areas. All employees receive extensive training to enable them to do this.

The purpose of the numbers is twofold. First, it focuses people's attention on what the company is about—making a profit. Profits are what lets the company live up to its mission statement: to provide good, secure jobs for people. SRC employees are remarkably focused on doing what needs to be done to make the company succeed, and they know just what that means for the particular job they do. Second, it creates the atmosphere of a game. Stack believes that people love to compete, even against their own standards. No one would want to play a game, however, if the score were kept secret.

One of the key financial issues all employees come to understand is price-to-earnings ratio. SRC stock has been valued at about 10 times earnings. Employees know that a dollar spent or earned is worth $10 down the road. So when employees were recently allowed to vote on whether to take a bonus payment when they just narrowly missed a target that would have triggered the bonus, they voted no.

Critical Numbers

In addition to stock, employees get a bonus of up to 13% to 18% of pay. The bonus has two parts. Half is based on profits and half on a "critical number." Each year, managers meet to determine a key weakness in the company. In 1991, it was improving the current ratio (current assets divided by current liabilities). All employees are taught what this is. Quarterly targets are set and bonuses paid based on meeting them. If they are not paid in a quarter, they can be paid in the next bonus period if the year-to-date numbers improve enough.

This split bonus helps people focus on the overall goal (profits) and on fixing problems. Stack notes that once the problem is fixed, and a new critical number is chosen, it has remained fixed. Things do not recede to previous levels absent the bonus.

Participation

Knowing all this information will not produce much unless employees can do something about it. So once a month employee "quality and productivity" teams meet to discuss ways to do things better. About 20% of the employees participate in these groups. Participation is voluntary, but the groups can ask for specific people to get involved if someone has special expertise. The teams can implement some ideas on their own; some require management approval.

Conclusion

All of this involvement places a lot of demands on employees. While plant-wide turnover is low (1.6% per year after people are in the ESOP), 75% of new employees leave in the first two months, almost all voluntarily. When employees come to work, they are told their job is 70% work and 30% thinking. Many people think that is just talk, but after 30 days, they are given their first 120-page financial statement and are told they will need to learn to read and understand it. Soon after, a lot of people leave.

For those who stay, however, the effort is worthwhile. The demands may be great, but so are the rewards.

W.L. Gore & Associates, Inc.

According to its own description, W.L. Gore & Associates is a company with "no titles, no bosses, and no special entitlements." Instead, its 7,000 "associates" (Gore is insistent it has no employees) form "multi-disciplined teams in plants of 200 or less, linked to other teams across the company." Instead of bosses or formal hierarchy, there are team leaders. These leaders are designated by the teams themselves by consensus; someone could be a team leader on one project and not on another. Gore's philosophy is that leadership should be based on abilities for that project, not on a position in a corporate structure. People are asked to work on projects. If they agree, then that is a "commitment" they must keep. There are no promotions, but people who make significant contributions to the company's success can get higher pay.

When hearing about Gore, most people react by saying "it can't really be true; there must be some de facto hierarchy." That skepticism is undermined, however, by the often reverential articles and case studies written by journalists and academics trained to be suspicious. No one has yet questioned whether the company really does what it says. The company regularly shows up on the *Best 100 Companies in America to Work For* list; *Fortune* said Gore was the epitome of what it called "post-heroic management"; and Ken Blanchard (author of *The One Minute Manager*) says he has never seen a company quite like Gore. Neither have we.

Background

W.L. Gore & Associates is best known as the manufacturer of Gore-Tex™ fabric, the breathable, waterproof material that revolutionized outdoor apparel. It makes a lot of other things based on this and related technology, however, including Glide™ dental floss, circuit board materials, clean room filters, surgical sutures, fiber optics, and many other products. Started in 1958, the company has had an annual compound growth rate in excess of 20% over the last 20 years. It has had a non-leveraged employee stock ownership plan (Associate Stock Ownership Plan, in Gore's terminology) since 1974. The ASOP was established with the primary objective of providing associates a mechanism to participate in the growth and success of the company through equity ownership. A majority of the stock is owned by working associates.

Gore was started when the late W.L. (Bill) Gore left Dupont to work on an application of Teflon material. Gore's philosophy of management was as important as the company's technological breakthroughs. The basic principles of that philosophy have guided the company since its inception:

- No fixed or assigned authority
- Sponsors, no bosses
- Natural leadership defined by followership
- Person-to-person communication
- Objectives set by those who must make them happen
- Tasks and functions organized through commitments

The resulting structure of management is organic rather than mechanical. There is responsibility and authority, but it will shift from person to person and team to team based on what the particular work demands and the skills and commitments people can make for that effort. To make this more practical, Gore limits its now almost 50 worldwide facilities to 200 people or fewer; having more employees per facility would impede easy communication.

How Work Flows

To understand what is going on, picture someone going to work at Gore. First, he or she is assigned a starting sponsor to help the associate get started. An advocate sponsor makes sure the associate gets credit and recognition, while a compensation sponsor makes sure the person is paid fairly. One person can fill all three roles.

Next, the associate makes commitments. A product specialist has an idea and creates a team by asking people around the plant if they want to participate (so without "followership," the leader has no project). The team may break into smaller teams, with team leaders emerging by consensus. Leaders may emerge based on technical skills, but creativity, the ability to work with others, and business judgment all are important as well. When the team is finished, it disbands and people make commitments to new projects. Compensation is determined by committees, and relies heavily on evaluations by other associates. Teams can draw their own budgets, provided it is not a "waterline" issue (one that threatens to sink the whole ship); then there must be discussion across teams and plants.

If all of this sounds somewhat ambiguous, it is, and intentionally so. More formal rules and procedures would inhibit risk taking and innovation. The trade-off may be that on some issues, Gore may make decisions more slowly or may not have everyone "on the same page" all the time. It is also a very demanding system for employees accustomed to more certainty. Companies like Gore, however, rise or fall based on their ability to create new ideas and applications. A structure that maximizes the ability of people to be creative has to sacrifice some of the orderliness that more traditional organizations have.

Further Reading

For more detail on this remarkable company, good articles can be found in Adolf Haasen and Gordon Shea, *A Better Place to Work* (American Management Association, 1997), "The New Post-Heroic Leadership," *Fortune* (February 21, 1994), and Frank Shipper and Charles Manz, "Employee Self-Management" (*Organizational Dynamics*, American Management Association, 1992). Gore-Tex™ is a registered trademark of W.L. Gore & Associates, Inc.

Yellow Springs Instruments

The center of the ESOP world is surely Yellow Springs, Ohio. The pleasant town of 5,000 people is best known as the home of Antioch College, but for us its real claim to fame is that all four of the town's major employers have ESOPs. No other place in America has so thoroughly adopted employee ownership as a way of doing business. The reasons for this phenomenon are not hard to find. The community's close-knit business leaders, many of whom are Antioch graduates, have shared their enthusiasm for the idea with each other. Yellow Springs and the college also have a long history of concern with social issues, and employee ownership has fit well into this broader outlook.

One of our first case studies at the NCEO was of one of the town's other ESOP companies, Antioch Publishing. Antioch's president, Lee Morgan, was one of those who suggested an ESOP to another major local company, Yellow Springs Instruments (YSI). YSI had a modest ESOP for many years, but in 1986, the company's ESOP bought 25% of the firm, while individual employees added another 30% to employee ownership. Since then, YSI has become a model for ways companies can integrate ESOPs into a corporate philosophy of employee involvement.

Company Background

YSI started in 1948 as a three-person organization located in the basement of an Antioch College science building. The founders were interested in developing measuring devices for a variety of markets. Today, YSI has 370 employees, some of whom work in the company's New

Mexico facility and also are in the ESOP. The company makes a variety of products for temperature measurement, including thermometers, sensors, and controllers for use in hospitals, airlines, space suits, satellites, and many other high-tech applications. A leader in environmental quality measurement, the company manufactures a variety of products in biological, medical, and other areas. Special applications can address individualized customer needs not met by standard products. YSI has pioneered a number of products, including the first practical electronic medical thermometers and the first practical heart-lung machine.

In short, the work demands a high degree of technological precision and sophistication, both in design and manufacturing. Careful, committed, and creative employees are essential to the company's success.

Starting the ESOP

The company's founders, Hardy Trolander and Dave Case, had always wanted the company to remain locally owned, and had established an ESOP that owned 10% of the stock. A committee elected by YSI workers served to handle employee problems and, to some extent, became a kind of bargaining agent for wages and working conditions. A profit-sharing plan provided contributions equal to about 5% of annual pay.

In the mid-80s, Trolander and Case were ready to retire. They brought in Malte von Matthiessen, an Antioch graduate, as president. Von Matthiessen had been working at NCR. While there, he had spent a considerable amount of time in Japan, and his experiences there, as well as his own readings and predilections, convinced him that if America were to compete, the talents of employees needed to be used more fully. Only a much broader ownership in companies and much more democratic participation in decisions, he believed, could accomplish this. Von Matthiessen was also on the board of Antioch Publishing, where he learned more about the potential of employee ownership.

Von Matthiessen told Tolander and Case that for him to become president, the two owners would have to commit to selling their remaining interests so that he could develop these themes with a free hand. In late 1986, an ESOP was started that will eventually own a majority of the stock.

Getting Owners Involved

As this was getting underway, the company began setting up a process to push decision making down to the lowest levels possible. The process has several components:

Training. Every employee is trained in team building. An initial group of employees was trained by professionals, and these employees now train their fellow employee owners. One person serves as the in-house expert. Another 40% of the employees have been trained in problem-solving techniques, again starting with an outside trainer who taught employees to run the program.

A new program to upgrade job skills is now getting started. An in-house person will lead the program, which will rely on employee mentors to teach their skills to other employees.

Participation at the job level. Currently, there are several standing employee committees to handle employee problems, social events, and ESOP communications. Ad hoc teams of employees are regularly formed to deal with issues as they arise. Sometimes managers choose these groups; sometimes they are formed by employees on their own. They may be within a single functional area, or they may overlap between different functions with representatives from each area.

The physical arrangement of the company also encourages communication. Everyone's work area, including managers, is organized with flexible dividers rather than formal offices. As von Matthiessen puts it, there would be an "open door" policy, but there are no doors.

These efforts are seen as just the start, and plans are underway to organize employees into groups of self-directing teams.

Participation beyond the job level. The company is planning to pass through full voting rights in the near future, partly because in a recent survey, employees said this was a matter of concern to them. A non-management employee may be added to the board, and various approaches are being considered to assure that every employee has a regular opportunity to meet with a board member. Historically, YSI has shared financial information with its employees.

A Company of Values

All of this reflects a commitment to core values developed by von Matthiessen and other employee owners. A copy of the values is regularly sent to customers as well as employees. Among the key elements of the value statement are these:

1. We cherish the customer.
2. We foster trust and a participative team process.
3. We are a company of individuals.
4. We foster effective leadership and communication.
5. We reward performance.
6. We encourage risk taking.
7. We are a dynamic organization.
8. We must grow to survive.

The company has continued to prosper as its ESOP has grown. Whether all the changes now underway will make a difference in the bottom line remains to be seen. The leadership and the employees at YSI, however, seem remarkably united in their assurance that this is the only way to proceed.

Ferrellgas

One of the largest ESOP transactions of the 1990s was the purchase by employees of 58% of Ferrellgas, the country's leading propane distributor. Ferrellgas operates in 45 states with over 5,000 employees and 650 retail outlets and satellite locations. A public company since 1994, Ferrellgas set up its ESOP in 1998 to buy out the interests of the family members who still owned a majority of the shares.

Today, the company is moving quickly to establish an employee ownership culture. In a commodity market like propane, companies have to distinguish themselves through superior service. The challenges have been particularly intense in the last two years as record warm winter temperatures have decreased propane demand and caused energy stock prices in general to decline sharply.

Company History

Ferrellgas was started in 1939 by A.C. Ferrell in Atchison, Kansas. Ferrell's son Jim has remained the company's chair since joining the business in 1965. At the time, Ferrellgas consisted of his father and one truck. The business grew quickly after that and now serves over one million residential, industrial, commercial, agricultural, and trade customers. Rural residential customers often rely on propane for most of their utility needs, while commercial customers use it for crop drying, space heating, irrigation, forklift operations, and other purposes.

Much of the company's growth has come through acquisitions. It recently acquired Thermogas, the country's fifth largest retailer, and in 1999 added 11 additional retail operations and their 32,000 customers. The company leads the industry in acquisitions and plans to look for new growth opportunities.

The 1994 public offering was unusual. The company was restructured in a master limited partnership, a kind of partnership arrangement in which partnership units are sold to the public instead of shares. The company consists of an operating partner, a limited partnership that encompasses the ownership of publicly traded units, and a general partner for overall management. The units trade on the New York Stock Exchange.

Creating the ESOP

The propane industry has been consolidating for years, and Jim Ferrell didn't want to see the family business sold to someone else. To provide a market for their shares, therefore, the company set up an ESOP that borrowed $160 million to make the purchase. Because the company was publicly traded, however, the sale did not qualify for capital gains tax deferral. The family could have sold to another company for its stock and deferred taxation, but there was a strong commitment to employees and the company's independence.

The ESOP is structured along conventional lines in terms of allocation, vesting, and other rules. For employees, the plan represents a significant improvement in benefits. Under the prior profit sharing plan, the company contributed 2% to 3% of employee pay; under the new plan, the company contribution has roughly tripled and employees should accumulate two to three times pay in stock value over 10 years if company targets are met. Employees continue to have a 401(k) plan, cafeteria plan, and other benefits.

Creating an Ownership Culture

The transition to an ownership culture will be an ongoing effort, made more challenging by the company's many locations. On the other hand, the company already had a flat management structure and an entrepreneurial spirit. Most local operations are small, with the typical facility having fewer than 10 employees. Local managers report directly to corporate headquarters, not to layers of regional or operational managers in between.

Two new programs were created after the ESOP to help jump start the ownership culture. SAFE (Sales Are for Everyone) is a training program to help employees learn better ways to sell Ferrellgas services. Employees are trained to track not just customers gained but the gross margins they generate as well. A variety of sales awards help provide incentive for the program.

In 1999, the company conducted a "cultural assessment" survey. Employees were asked their opinions on how to improve operations in a variety of areas. Management is now studying the responses. Employees also all got bumper stickers announcing Ferrellgas is employee owned, and the company is highlighting the fact in its marketing materials.

Early Results

Some early results suggest that the new ESOP is having an impact. Turnover dropped 20% compared to the previous year, despite the tight job market. Workers' compensation rates set record lows. Earnings before interest, taxes, and depreciation rose 15% over 1998, and net earnings before extraordinary charges rose from $4.9 million in 1998 to $14.8 million in 1999. These results were obtained despite record warm winter temperatures.

As one of a handful of companies with over 1,000 employees to convert to majority ESOP status in the 1990s, the progress of Ferrellgas could be an important marker for other companies that look to employee ownership as an alternative to being sold, or to going or remaining public.

About the Authors

Edward J. Carberry is a graduate student in sociology at Cornell University. At the time he wrote his chapter in this book, he was the senior project director at the National Center for Employee Ownership (NCEO), where he wrote and edited publications, conducted research, and facilitated educational seminars on various topics relating to employee ownership. He is the author or co-author of several publications on employee ownership and participation, and also has authored many articles on employee ownership for business and trade publications. Mr. Carberry holds a Bachelor of Arts degree from Bates College in Lewiston, Maine.

John J. Cresto is a partner in the Chicago office of the law firm Seyfarth Shaw. He has advised corporations and their shareholders and directors regarding financing options in ESOP transactions. In addition, Mr. Cresto has served as legal counsel to many banks and other lenders and to trustees in ESOP transactions. Mr. Cresto is a member of the ESOP Association and is a member of its National Finance Committee. Mr. Cresto also is a member of the NCEO. He regularly makes presentations regarding ESOPs and ESOP financing at seminars, including the annual national conventions of the ESOP Association and the NCEO.

Ronald J. Gilbert is the co-founder and president of ESOP Services, Inc., in Scottsville, VA. With over 20 years of ESOP experience, he serves as a director of several ESOP companies and on the board of governors of the ESOP Association and is a coauthor of *Employee Stock Ownership Plans: Business Planning, Implementation, Law and Taxation*.

Anthony I. Mathews is a consultant and principal with BCI Group. BCI is a full-service, nationally recognized leader in the area of employee benefits consulting and administration specializing in ESOPs and other complex defined contribution and defined benefit plans. BCI has 9 offices around the U.S., with headquarters in Appleton, Wisconsin. Tony works out of the Los Angeles office, and he brings to the practice more than 20 years of experience as an ESOP consultant and administrator.

Scott Rodrick is the director of publishing and information technology at the National Center for Employee Ownership (NCEO). Mr. Rodrick created and maintains the NCEO's Web sites and is the author of the NCEO's booklet *An Introduction to ESOPs* (rev. 4th ed. 2002), the editor and or/coauthor of various other NCEO publications, and the coeditor of *Employee Stock Ownership Plans* (Harcourt Brace, 1996, 1999). He served at the U.S. Department of Labor as an attorney-advisor before coming to the NCEO.

Corey Rosen is the founder and executive director of the National Center for Employee Ownership (NCEO). He is the author or coauthor of many NCEO publications, five books from commercial publishers, and over 100 articles on employee ownership for a variety of professional, academic, and trade publications. He has lectured on the subject across the world and met with government, business, and union leaders. Mr. Rosen received his Ph.D. from Cornell University in political science in 1973, taught government at Ripon College, and then served as a Senate staff member until 1981, when he cofounded the NCEO. As a Senate staffer, he helped draft some of the current ESOP legislation.

Andrew Sandquist is an investment specialist with CB Richard Ellis' Investment Properties Group in Oak Brook, Illinois. As a senior member of the Investment Properties Group, Mr. Sandquist specializes in the placement of single-tenant net leased industrials and sale-leaseback investment offerings throughout North America. At the time he coauthored "Anticipating and Avoiding ESOP Financing Obstacles," he was the director of corporate finance at Prairie Capital Advisors, where he structured exit strategies for owners of middle market manufacturing companies and owners of commercial real estate.

About the NCEO

The National Center for Employee Ownership (NCEO) is widely considered to be "the single best source of information on employee ownership anywhere in the world" (*Inc.* magazine). Established in 1981 as a nonprofit information and membership organization, the NCEO now has over 3,000 members, including companies, professionals, unions, government officials, academics, and others. It is funded entirely through the work it does. The NCEO publishes a variety of materials explaining how employee ownership plans work, describing how to get employees more involved, and reviewing the research in this field. The NCEO also holds dozens of seminars and conferences annually.

NCEO Membership. NCEO members receive (1) the bimonthly newsletter *Employee Ownership Report,* which covers both ESOPs and stock options; (2) access to the members-only area of the NCEO Web site (*www.nceo.org*), including a searchable database of over 200 service providers; (3) discounts on NCEO publications and events; and (4) the right to telephone the NCEO for answers to general or specific questions regarding employee ownership. It costs $80 to join the NCEO for one year; see the order form on the next page.

NCEO Publications. This book, *The ESOP Reader,* is $25 for NCEO members and $35 for nonmembers. Other books that might interest readers include *Selling to an ESOP, Leveraged ESOPs and Employee Buyouts,* and *ESOP Valuation,* all of which also are $25 and $35 each. See *www.nceo.org* for more information.

Order Form

To order, fill out this form and mail it with your credit card information or check to the NCEO at 1736 Franklin Street, 8th Floor, Oakland, CA 94612; fax it with your credit card information to the NCEO at 510-272-9510; telephone us at 510-208-1300 with your credit card in hand; or order securely online at our Web site, *www.nceo.org.* If you are not already a member, you can join now to receive member discounts on any publications you order.

Name

Organization

Address

City, State, Zip (Country)

Telephone   Fax   E-mail

Method of Payment: ❏ Check (payable to "NCEO") ❏ Visa ❏ M/C ❏ AMEX

Credit Card Number

Signature   Exp. Date

Checks are accepted only for orders from the U.S. and must be in U.S. currency.

Title	Qty.	Price	Total

Tax: California residents add 8.25% sales tax (on publications only, not membership)	Subtotal $
Shipping: In the U.S., first publication $5, each add'l $1; elsewhere, we charge exact shipping costs to your credit card, plus (except for Canada) a $10 handling surcharge; no shipping charges for membership	Sales Tax $
	Shipping $
Introductory NCEO Membership: $80 for one year ($90 outside the U.S.)	Membership $
	TOTAL DUE $